FEDERAL
INDIAN POLICY

Lake Superior

MICHIGAN

Lake Huron

WISCONSIN

Lake Michigan

Samuel de Champlain, French, 1609

Jacques Cartier, French, 1534

MAINE

Abenaki

VERMONT

NEW HAMPSHIRE

Probably Norse fishermen, late 15th century

Huron

Lake Ontario

Lake Erie

Iroquois

NEW YORK

MASSACHUSETTS

Wampanoag

RHODE ISLAND

Narragansett

CONNECTICUT

Giovanni da Verrazano, Italian, 1524

ILLINOIS

INDIANA

OHIO

PENNSYLVANIA

MARYLAND

NEW JERSEY

Lenape

DELAWARE

WEST VIRGINIA

VIRGINIA

Nanticoke

John Smith, English, 1608

KENTUCKY

Powhatan Tribes

Probably Spanish explorers, 1520s

TENNESSEE

Catawba

NORTH CAROLINA

Cherokee

SOUTH CAROLINA

Lumbee

Chickasaw

Upper Creek

Choctaw

GEORGIA

ALABAMA

Hernando de Soto, Spanish, 1540

MISSISSIPPI

Lower Creek

ATLANTIC

OCEAN

FLORIDA

Seminole (Calusa)

Ponce de León, Spanish, 1521

GULF OF MEXICO

FEDERAL INDIAN POLICY

Lawrence C. Kelly
University of North Texas, Denton

Frank W. Porter III
General Editor

CHELSEA HOUSE PUBLISHERS
New York   Philadelphia

On the cover A dance performed by Shoshone Indians, painted on muslin by Charles Washakie in the late 19th century.

Chelsea House Publishers
Editor-in-Chief Nancy Toff
Executive Editor Remmel T. Nunn
Managing Editor Karyn Gullen Browne
Copy Chief Juliann Barbato
Picture Editor Adrian G. Allen
Art Director Maria Epes
Manufacturing Manager Gerald Levine

Indians of North America
Senior Editor Liz Sonneborn

Staff For **FEDERAL INDIAN POLICY**
Associate Editor Clifford W. Crouch
Deputy Copy Chief Nicole Bowen
Copy Editor Philip Koslow
Editorial Assistant Claire Wilson
Assistant Art Director Loraine Machlin
Designer Donna Sinisgalli
Design Assistant James Baker
Picture Researcher Margalit Fox
Production Manager Joseph Romano
Production Coordinator Marie Claire Cebrián

5 7 9 8 6 4

Library of Congress Cataloging-in-Publication Data

Kelly, Lawrence C.
    Federal Indian Policy / Lawrence C. Kelly.
        p.   cm.—(Indians of North America)
    Summary: Traces the history of the development of U.S. policy concerning American Indians.
    ISBN 1-55546-706-7
        0-7910-0381-7 (pbk.)
    Bibliography: p.
    Includes index.
    1. Indians of North America—Government relations.
    2. Indians, Treatment of—United States.   [1. Indians of North America—Government relations.   2. Indians—Treatment.] I. Title. II. Series: Indians of North America (Chelsea House Publishers)
                                                                89-9980
E93.K297   1989   CIP
323.1'197—dc20   AC

CONTENTS

INDIANS OF NORTH AMERICA

The Abenaki

The Apache

The Arapaho

The Archaeology
  of North America

The Aztecs

The Blackfoot

The Cahuilla

The Catawbas

The Cherokee

The Cheyenne

The Chickasaw

The Chinook

The Chipewyan

The Choctaw

The Chumash

The Coast Salish Peoples

The Comanche

The Creeks

The Crow

Federal Indian Policy

The Hidatsa

The Hopi

The Huron

The Innu

The Inuit

The Iroquois

The Kiowa

The Kwakiutl

The Lenapes

Literatures of the
  American Indian

The Lumbee

The Maya

The Menominee

The Modoc

The Mohawk

The Nanticoke

The Narragansett

The Navajos

The Nez Perce

The Ojibwa

The Osage

The Paiute

The Pawnee

The Pima-Maricopa

The Potawatomi

The Powhatan Tribes

The Pueblo

The Quapaws

The Sac and Fox

The Santee Sioux

The Seminole

The Shawnee

The Shoshone

The Tarahumara

The Teton Sioux

The Tunica-Biloxi

Urban Indians

The Wampanoag

Women in American
  Indian Society

The Yakima

The Yankton Sioux

The Yuma

The Zuni

CHELSEA HOUSE PUBLISHERS

INDIANS OF NORTH AMERICA: CONFLICT AND SURVIVAL

Frank W. Porter III

The Indians survived our open intention of wiping them out, and since the tide turned they have even weathered our good intentions toward them, which can be much more deadly.

John Steinbeck
America and Americans

When Europeans first reached the North American continent, they found hundreds of tribes occupying a vast and rich country. The newcomers quickly recognized the wealth of natural resources. They were not, however, so quick or willing to recognize the spiritual, cultural, and intellectual riches of the people they called Indians.

The Indians of North America examines the problems that develop when people with different cultures come together. For American Indians, the consequences of their interaction with non-Indian people have been both productive and tragic. The Europeans believed they had "discovered" a "New World," but their religious bigotry, cultural bias, and materialistic world view kept them from appreciating and understanding the people who lived in it. All too often they attempted to change the way of life of the indigenous people. The Spanish conquistadores wanted the Indians as a source of labor. The Christian missionaries, many of whom were English, viewed them as potential converts. French traders and trappers used the Indians as a means to obtain pelts. As Francis Parkman, the 19th-century historian, stated, "Spanish civilization crushed the Indian; English civilization scorned and neglected him; French civilization embraced and cherished him."

7

Nearly 500 years later, many people think of American Indians as curious vestiges of a distant past, waging a futile war to survive in a Space Age society. Even today, our understanding of the history and culture of American Indians is too often derived from unsympathetic, culturally biased, and inaccurate reports. The American Indian, described and portrayed in thousands of movies, television programs, books, articles, and government studies, has either been raised to the status of the "noble savage" or disparaged as the "wild Indian" who resisted the westward expansion of the American frontier.

Where in this popular view are the real Indians, the human beings and communities whose ancestors can be traced back to ice-age hunters? Where are the creative and indomitable people whose sophisticated technologies used the natural resources to ensure their survival, whose military skill might even have prevented European settlement of North America if not for devastating epidemics and disruption of the ecology? Where are the men and women who are today diligently struggling to assert their legal rights and express once again the value of their heritage?

The various Indian tribes of North America, like people everywhere, have a history that includes population expansion, adaptation to a range of regional environments, trade across wide networks, internal strife, and warfare. This was the reality. Europeans justified their conquests, however, by creating a mythical image of the New World and its native people. In this myth, the New World was a virgin land, waiting for the Europeans. The arrival of Christopher Columbus ended a timeless primitiveness for the original inhabitants.

Also part of this myth was the debate over the origins of the American Indians. Fantastic and diverse answers were proposed by the early explorers, missionairies, and settlers. Some thought that the Indians were descended from the Ten Lost Tribes of Israel, others that they were descended from inhabitants of the lost continent of Atlantis. One writer suggested that the Indians had reached North America in another Noah's ark.

A later myth, perpetrated by many historians, focused on the relentless persecution during the past five centuries until only a scattering of these "primitive" people remained to be herded onto reservations. This view fails to chronicle the overt and covert ways in which the Indians successfully coped with the intruders.

All of these myths presented one-sided interpretations that ignored the complexity of European and American events and policies. All left serious questions unanswered. What were the origins of the American Indians? Where did they come from? How and when did they get to the New World? What was their life—their culture—really like?

In the late 1800s, anthropologists and archaeologists in the Smithsonian Institution's newly created Bureau of American Ethnology in Washington,

D.C., began to study scientifically the history and culture of the Indians of North America. They were motivated by an honest belief that the Indians were on the verge of extinction and that along with them would vanish their languages, religious beliefs, technology, myths, and legends. These men and women went out to visit, study, and record data from as many Indian communities as possible before this information was forever lost.

By this time there was a new myth in the national consciousness. American Indians existed as figures in the American past. They had performed a historical mission. They had challenged white settlers who trekked across the continent. Once conquered, however, they were supposed to accept graciously the way of life of their conquerors.

The reality again was different. American Indians resisted both actively and passively. They refused to lose their unique identity, to be assimilated into white society. Many whites viewed the Indians not only as members of a conquered nation but also as "inferior" and "unequal." The rights of the Indians could be expanded, contracted, or modified as the conquerors saw fit. In every generation, white society asked itself what to do with the American Indians. Their answers have resulted in the twists and turns of federal Indian policy.

There were two general approaches. One way was to raise the Indians to a "higher level" by "civilizing" them. Zealous missionaries considered it their Christian duty to elevate the Indian through conversion and scanty education. The other approach was to ignore the Indians until they disappeared under pressure from the ever-expanding white society. The myth of the "vanishing Indian" gave stronger support to the latter option, helping to justify the taking of the Indians' land.

Prior to the end of the 18th century, there was no national policy on Indians simply because the American nation has not yet come into existence. American Indians similarly did not possess a political or social unity with which to confront the various Europeans. They were not homogeneous. Rather, they were loosely formed bands and tribes, speaking nearly 300 languages and thousands of dialects. The collective identity felt by Indians today is a result of their common experiences of defeat and/or mistreatment at the hands of whites.

During the colonial period, the British crown did not have a coordinated policy toward the Indians of North America. Specific tribes (most notably the Iroquois and the Cherokee) became military and political pawns used by both the crown and the individual colonies. The success of the American Revolution brought no immediate change. When the United States acquired new territory from France and Mexico in the early 19th century, the federal government wanted to open this land to settlement by homesteaders. But the Indian tribes that lived on this land had signed treaties with European governments assuring their title to the land. Now the United States assumed legal responsibility for honoring these treaties.

At first, President Thomas Jefferson believed that the Louisiana Purchase contained sufficient land for both the Indians and the white population. Within a generation, though, it became clear that the Indians would not be allowed to remain. In the 1830s the federal government began to coerce the eastern tribes to sign treaties agreeing to relinquish their ancestral land and move west of the Mississippi River. Whenever these negotiations failed, President Andrew Jackson used the military to remove the Indians. The southeastern tribes, promised food and transportation during their removal to the West, were instead forced to walk the "Trail of Tears." More than 4,000 men, woman, and children died during this forced march. The "removal policy" was successful in opening the land to homesteaders, but it created enormous hardships for the Indians.

By 1871 most of the tribes in the United States had signed treaties ceding most or all of their ancestral land in exchange for reservations and welfare. The treaty terms were intended to bind both parties for all time. But in the General Allotment Act of 1887, the federal government changed its policy again. Now the goal was to make tribal members into individual landowners and farmers, encouraging their absorption into white society. This policy was advantageous to whites who were eager to acquire Indian land, but it proved disastrous for the Indians. One hundred thirty-eight million acres of reservation land were subdivided into tracts of 160, 80, or as little as 40 acres, and allotted tribe members on an individual basis. Land owned in this way was said to have "trust status" and could not be sold. But the surplus land—all Indian land not allotted to individuals—was opened (for sale) to white settlers. Ultimately, more than 90 million acres of land were taken from the Indians by legal and illegal means.

The resulting loss of land was a catastrophe for the Indians. It was necessary to make it illegal for Indians to sell their land to non-Indians. The Indian Reorganization Act of 1934 officially ended the allotment period. Tribes that voted to accept the provisions of this act were reorganized, and an effort was made to purchase land within preexisting reservations to restore an adequate land base.

Ten years later, in 1944, federal Indian policy again shifted. Now the federal government wanted to get out of the "Indian business." In 1953 an act of Congress named specific tribes whose trust status was to be ended "at the earliest possible time." This new law enabled the United States to end unilaterally, whether the Indians wished it or not, the special status that protected the land in Indian tribal reservations. In the 1950s federal Indian policy was to transfer federal responsibility and jurisdiction to state governments, encourage the physical relocation of Indian peoples from reservations to urban areas, and hasten the termination, or extinction, of tribes.

Between 1954 and 1962 Congress passed specific laws authorizing the termination of more than 100 tribal groups. The stated purpose of the termination policy was to ensure the full and complete integration of Indians into American society. However, there is a less benign way to interpret this legislation. Even as termination was being discussed in Congress, 133 separate bills were introduced to permit the transfer of trust land ownership from Indians to non-Indians.

With the Johnson administration in the 1960s the federal government began to reject termination. In the 1970s yet another Indian policy emerged. Known as "self-determination," it favored keeping the protective role of the federal government while increasing tribal participation in, and control of, important areas of local government. In 1983 President Reagan, in a policy statement on Indian affairs, restated the unique "government is government" relationship of the United States with the Indians. However, federal programs since then have moved toward transferring Indian affairs to individual states, which have long desired to gain control of Indian land and resources.

As long as American Indians retain power, land, and resources that are coveted by the states and the federal government, there will continue to be a "clash of cultures," and the issues will be contested in the courts, Congress, the White House, and even in the international human rights community. To give all Americans a greater comprehension of the issues and conflicts involving American Indians today is a major goal of this series. These issues are not easily understood, nor can these conflicts be readily resolved. The study of North American Indian history and culture is a necessary and important step toward that comprehension. All Americans must learn the history of the relations between the Indians and the federal government, recognize the unique legal status of the Indians, and understand the heritage and cultures of the Indians of North America.

American artist Edward Hicks's 1835 painting of William Penn, the founder of Pennsylvania, meeting with a group of Indians in 1682.

COLONIAL
INDIAN POLICY
1492 TO 1776

In the fall of 1859, prospectors flocked into the territory of Colorado in search of gold, which had been discovered in the Rocky Mountains. The sudden influx of non-Indians alarmed the Cheyenne and Arapaho, Indian tribes that lived in this area. They survived by hunting the large herds of buffalo that roamed the flatlands of what are now Kansas and Colorado, and now these herds were being scattered by the newcomers. The Indians were further angered by the settlers, who soon followed the prospectors to their territory, cleared their land, and built towns on its choicest sites.

Rather than attack the settlers, the Cheyenne, the Arapaho, and a third group of Indians, the Sioux, negotiated a treaty with Thomas S. Twiss, a representative of the Bureau of Indian Affairs (BIA), the U.S. government agency responsible for dealing with Indians.

This treaty ceded a vast area of these Indians' lands—stretching from present-day North Dakota to Kansas—to the United States. In return, the Indians received a much smaller tract in what is now southeastern Wyoming and were promised a yearly payment, or annuity, of $16,000. They knew that the United States got the better of the deal, but, outmanned by the large and heavily armed U.S. forces, the Indians were willing to settle for a plot of land where they would be left in peace.

The crisis continued, however. Other Indians held out against the whites, some fighting pitched battles against the U.S. Army. Often those Indians who quietly agreed to live on reservations were cheated out of their annuities or denied the provisions they had been promised. Eventually, the conflicts would lead to congressional investigations and to Supreme Court rulings. Even then, problems would persist. More than a century later, Indians throughout the country would still find themselves at odds with whites, and the legality of agreements made between them would continue to be hotly disputed.

The conflicts between Indians and whites in the United States have a long history. Almost immediately after it was formed, the U.S. government recognized that Indians lived on most of its land and that arrangements had to be made with them to keep conflicts to a minimum. However, whites and Indians found when dealing with each other that their cultures were very different. These differences created misunderstandings, and these misunderstandings, then as now, would doom many of the United States's Indian policies.

The origin of these misguided policies can be traced back to the attitudes and prejudices of the first Europeans who, starting in the 16th century, began to settle in North America. They quickly formed two views of the native inhabitants they met. One view, based on friendly dealings with Indians, held that they were simple, trusting "children of nature," free of civilization and its vices. The other view, based on the contact some Europeans had with peoples who resisted invasion, held that the Indians were bloodthirsty, deceptive, and treacherous. Opposed as these views seem, they were alike in two important ways. First, both were crude exaggerations—stereotypes. Sec-

ond, both stemmed from the Europeans' belief in their superiority to the Indians.

The European image of the Indians was further colored by a theological debate. Early explorers reported that the natives were like themselves in some respects but considerably different in other ways. Among Europeans the question arose as to whether the natives were truly human or whether they were members of a subhuman species. The answer was important because it would determine whether the natives could be exploited without guilt and whether it was necessary or desirable to convert them to Christianity. After many years of scholarly debate, Europeans concluded that Indians were in fact human beings, but because of the cultural gap that existed between Indians and Europeans, many of the whites' exploitative attitudes lingered.

Probably the greatest such gap was the difference between European and Indian concepts of land. From the outset of their contact, the two societies held sharply divergent views that left no room for compromise. Europeans thought of land as a commodity that could be owned by individuals and bought or sold. Indians, on the other hand, believed that specific areas of land were to be used exclusively by the people who occupied them. All these people had a right to the land's resources (although not necessarily in equal portions), and no single individual owned a specific part of the group's territory.

The way Europeans and Indians were organized politically and socially also differed sharply. The inhabitants of the European countries that founded colonies in North America—such as Spain, France, and England—considered themselves the subjects of a single monarch and the citizens of a distinct nation. As such, they had a sense of unity and shared purpose. Although all North American Indians had certain cultural traits in common, they were not a united people in the sense that the Spanish or the English were. Indians were divided into hundreds of tribes, societies of people who felt bound to

This ballad, which was written in 1623 by an English colonist, describes the recovery of the Virginia colony after the murder of 330 settlers by Pamunkey Indians. Broadsides such as this provided the English public with much of their knowledge of the British colonies in North America.

TRADITIONAL HOMELANDS OF MAJOR INDIAN TRIBES

AT CONTACT WITH EUROPEANS IN THE 16TH CENTURY

Ojibwa

Dakota
(Sioux)

Lake Superior

Abenaki

Menominee

Lake
Huron

Lake
Michigan

Huron

Lake Ontario

Iroquois

Sac
and
Fox

Potawatomi

Wampanoag

Narragansett

Lake Erie

Lenape

Illinois

Miami

Nanticoke

Missouri

Powhatan
Tribes

Osage

Shawnee

Catawba

Cherokee

Lumbee

ATLANTIC

OCEAN

Quapaw

Upper Creek

Wichita

Choctaw
Chickasaw

Tunica

Lower Creek

Biloxi

Seminole
(Calusa)

GULF OF MEXICO

(modern state boundaries)

each other by a common history, kinship, and language. Tribes living in different parts of North America had very different ways of life. The Cherokee, for instance, who lived in the woodlands of what is now the southeastern United States, no more resembled the Cheyenne, who lived on the Plains, than the British resembled the Spanish or French. Indeed, so distinct were the various peoples and so often were they at odds that the Indian population of North America never banded together to battle the white intruders who would eventually overrun their lands.

The first nation to colonize North America was Spain, in the 16th century. Spanish conquistadores (conquerors) cruelly exploited the native civilizations of Mexico and South America, such as the Aztecs and Mayans. But farther north, on the frontiers of Spain's colonies (known as New Spain), the Spanish recognized the rights of settled, peaceful agricultural Indians to their land and granted them legal title—or claim—to it that was binding in Spanish law. This was true especially in the Rio Grande area of present-day New Mexico.

In other areas, including what are now California, Arizona, and Texas, the Spanish gathered peaceful bands and tribes into missions, organizations run by priests who tried to convert the Indians to the Roman Catholic faith. The Spaniards also gave the Indians title to the land they inhabited. Even today, Indians such as the Rio Grande Pueblo, whose land titles were confirmed by

Spain, have generally managed to retain them over the protests of nearby whites.

The Spanish seldom tried to replace local Indian leaders. Instead they worked with them and recognized a right to sovereignty or tribal self-government for many of the peoples they met. The Apache, for instance, coexisted peacefully with the Spanish in the early 17th century. Apache visited trading posts set up by the colonists and swapped buffalo hides for grain, cattle, and—prized above all—horses. The relationship soured when the Spanish began enslaving Apache, whom they hunted down like beasts. Thereafter, the two peoples were at war.

Yet Spanish policy toward the Indians had some admirable features. Spanish explorers believed that all the land they discovered belonged to their king. The king, in turn, believed that every person living in the colonies, including Indians, was his subject and thus entitled to royal protection. For this reason, Spanish kings decreed laws for the settlement and governance of the colonies, laws that provided for the protection of Indian rights. These laws were not always obeyed by colonists, but they provided grounds for the Indians' supporters, such as clergymen, to make formal appeals for better treatment.

A second European power, France, founded its first North American colony almost a century later than Spain. Settled in 1608, the colony was Quebec in New France (Canada). Like the Spanish, the French based their colonial policy on the concept that their colonies were owned by the king and that all who lived within them were his subjects. Unlike Spain, however, France did not formally recognize Indian land titles. The French were less concerned with land rights, because most of them were traders, not settlers. Their goal in traveling to North America was to acquire furs that they could sell in European markets for high prices. Most French remained on the continent for only short periods of time and then returned to France.

Like the Spanish, the French enlisted the aid of Indian leaders rather than impose political or military control over them. The French also early adopted the Indian custom of exchanging gifts to win Indian support. These measures benefited the French and the Indians alike. The French won many allies among the Indians—including the Abenaki, Algonquin, and Huron in the Northeast—and, as a result, were able to exert their influence over a much larger area than their small numbers would otherwise have allowed.

The least charitable Indian policy—and the forerunner of American policy—was devised by England. The English came to North America in relatively large numbers, primarily seeking land for their families. Some groups, such as the Pilgrims who founded Plymouth Colony in present-day Massachusetts in 1620, were fleeing religious persecution in their homeland. Others, such as those who in 1607

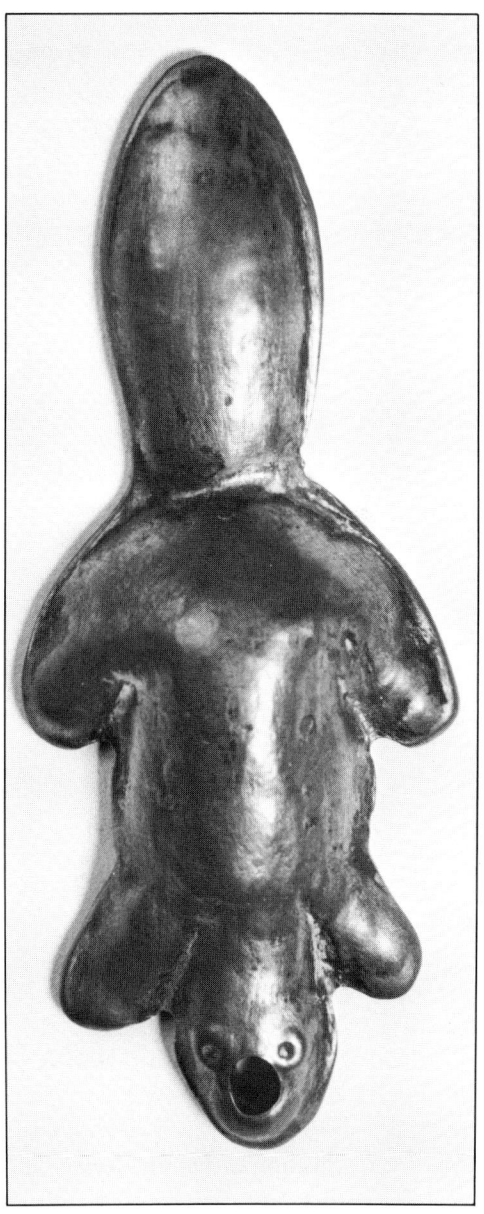

A copper token, in the shape of a beaver, that was used in the 17th-century fur trade between the French and the Indians in present-day Canada. This token was equal in value to one beaver fur.

settled Jamestown, Virginia, the first enduring British colony, came to seek their fortune through trade and agriculture. In both cases, the colonists intended to make a permanent home in North America. As the population of the English colonists grew, so did the need for more land. The English soon came to view the Indians as a barrier to expansion. Relations between the colonists and the Indians were not eased by the harsh religious beliefs of the English, especially the Puritans, who had little use even for their fellow Christians in England.

There was yet another reason for conflict. Unlike the Spanish and French monarchs, who wanted to extend their rule to their colonies, the English kings, at least in the beginning, showed little interest in the lands claimed in their name by their subjects. Instead, the English kings tended to offer land to citizens they wanted to reward or placate. Jamestown, for instance, was settled by a group of merchants who prevailed upon the king to grant them a portion of his land for the purpose of developing trade and commerce. Colonies in the Carolinas, Pennsylvania, and Maryland were awarded to individuals to whom the king was indebted.

Founded under various circumstances, the colonies evolved independently from one another. Indeed, until the colonists declared their independence from England in 1776 and formed their own central government, each of the 13 colonies was governed in a dif-

An 18th-century engraving of Sachem, the 70-year-old Mohawk chief who led 200 British-allied Indian warriors in battle against the French during the French and Indian War. At the Battle of Lake George in 1755, Sachem and most of the members of his detachment were killed by French musketeers.

ferent way and according to different principles. Consequently, each colony evolved its own Indian policy. This fact was not lost on the Indians, who saw the English as the greatest threat to their survival and well-being.

In Connecticut, Massachusetts, and Virginia, the English tried to drive out the Indians soon after settling. Other colonies, Rhode Island and Pennsylvania in particular, initially adopted much more enlightened policies toward the natives. Roger Williams, who founded Rhode Island, and William Penn, who owned Pennsylvania, forbade colonists to take Indian lands without permission or without giving compensation. But after Williams's death in 1683 and Penn's in 1718, their colonies also began to coerce the Indians to give up lands that whites wanted.

From 1607 to the mid-1700s, English settlers remained in the coastal and foothill areas of the Atlantic seaboard. This area, primarily covered with dense forest, was difficult to farm. Before a family could begin to raise crops on a plot of land, it had to cut down all the trees and clear away the stumps—tasks that could take several years to complete. The colonists might have ventured farther inland in search of more hospitable land, but they were penned in by the Appalachian Mountains. So they stayed put—and multiplied. By the 1740s, their population reached about 1.5 million, far more inhabitants than French or Spanish colonies in North America, and probably more than the Indian communities in the vicinity of the English settlements.

Eventually the English colonists ran out of land to settle east of the Appalachians, and they began to eye the uncharted land directly to the west of the mountain range. But the English could move there only at the expense of the many Indian groups who inhabited the region and of the French fur traders who dealt with them.

When the colonization of North America began, the three European powers had managed to stay out of each other's way—the new continent was large enough to satisfy them all. But as early as 1689, France and England skirmished in North America. These battles were part of a much larger, worldwide struggle between two of the greatest empires in the world. At first the skirmishes involved settlers. As French colonists moved southward from Canada, they clashed with English settlers moving west from the seaboard. The English, whose colonies had a much larger population, usually won. But these victories were hard won and costly because the French had learned guerrilla tactics from their Indian allies.

The rivalry between England and France heated up in 1754, when the conflict popularly known in the English colonies as the French and Indian War began. In that year, the French built Fort Duquesne (the site of the present-day city of Pittsburgh, Pennsylvania) at the headwaters of the Ohio River. The English colony of Virginia also laid claim to this area and sent its militia, headed by a 22-year-old army officer, George Washington, to do battle with the French. The French defeated the militia twice, and Washington was forced to surrender. Months later, troops arrived from England, but again the French won with the assistance of their Indian allies.

EASTERN NORTH AMERICA, 1763

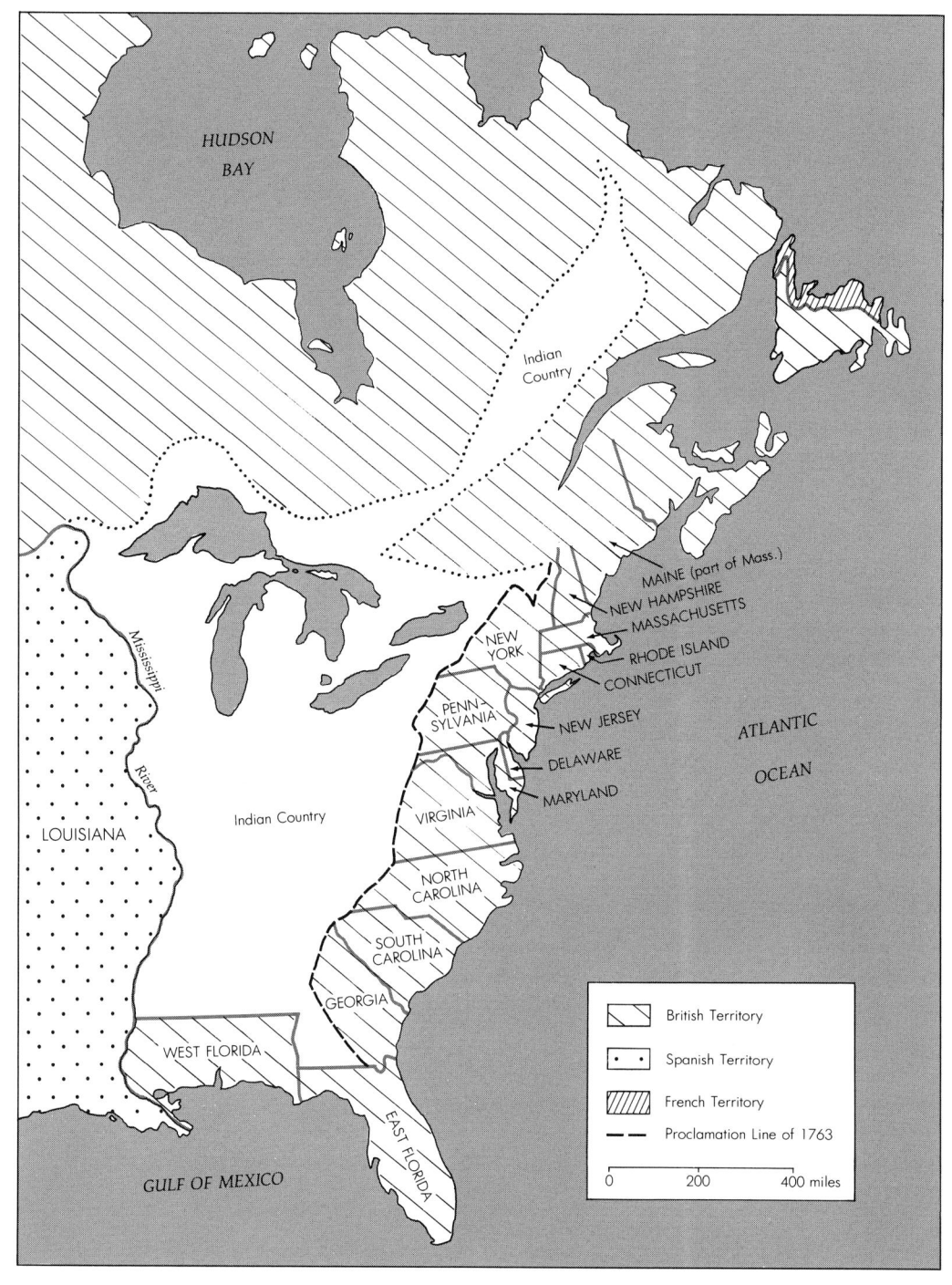

HUDSON
BAY

Indian
Country

MAINE (part of Mass.)
NEW HAMPSHIRE
MASSACHUSETTS
RHODE ISLAND
CONNECTICUT

NEW
YORK

PENN-
SYLVANIA

NEW JERSEY

DELAWARE

MARYLAND

VIRGINIA

ATLANTIC

OCEAN

Mississippi

River

Indian Country

LOUISIANA

NORTH
CAROLINA

SOUTH
CAROLINA

GEORGIA

WEST FLORIDA

EAST FLORIDA

GULF OF MEXICO

British Territory

Spanish Territory

French Territory

Proclamation Line of 1763

0   200   400 miles

The French won several more early clashes, and English settlers in New York, Pennsylvania, Maryland, Virginia, and the Carolinas lived in fear of sudden attack from the French and Indians. As the war dragged on, both England and France sent troops and supplies to their colonies. England sent more, however, and France could not afford to match its rival. In 1763 the Treaty of Paris recognized Great Britain as the owner of all the land from Canada to Spanish Florida and from the Atlantic Ocean to the Mississippi River.

When the French surrendered, they made no provisions for their Indian allies. Those who lived along the Ohio River and in the Great Lakes area fully recognized that an English victory meant that they might lose their land, so they banded together under a remarkable leader, an Ottawa named Pontiac, and prepared to resist the English takeover. In 1763 and 1764, Pontiac's forces overran most of the English forts west of the Appalachians, to the alarm of the British military commanders and the settlers who had begun to move into the area surrendered by France. But despite their victories, the Indians gradually gave way to the colonists. Pontiac's army failed in part because his followers came from many different tribes; therefore, it was hard for them to subordinate their differences to the task of defeating a common foe. Many Indians also withdrew to plant spring crops.

The British, however, were so impressed with the savagery and skill of Pontiac's forces that they formulated a new, uniform Indian policy. The Proclamation of 1763 established a line, roughly corresponding to the crest of the Appalachian Mountains, that no English settlers could cross until representatives of the government negotiated treaties and land cessions with the Indians living there. In theory, the Proclamation Line assured the Indians that they would be secure in their lands until they were willing to sell them to the British government.

The document implied something even more important—that Indian nations were independent and that none of their lands would be taken without their permission or without compensation. This meant, in addition, that the individual British colonies would no longer deal directly with the Indians. Instead, Indian relations would be regulated by the central English government in London through agents, people who would be appointed specifically to coordinate Indian policy.

The scheme sounded better than it actually proved to be. The colonists had little use for a plan hatched across the ocean by a government they themselves often contested. Although England appointed two agents to carry out its new policy, their efforts had no opportunity to become effective. Disregarding the Proclamation Line, land-hungry settlers soon crossed the Appalachian Mountains and poured into what are now western Pennsylvania and Kentucky. The stage was set for new conflicts. ▲

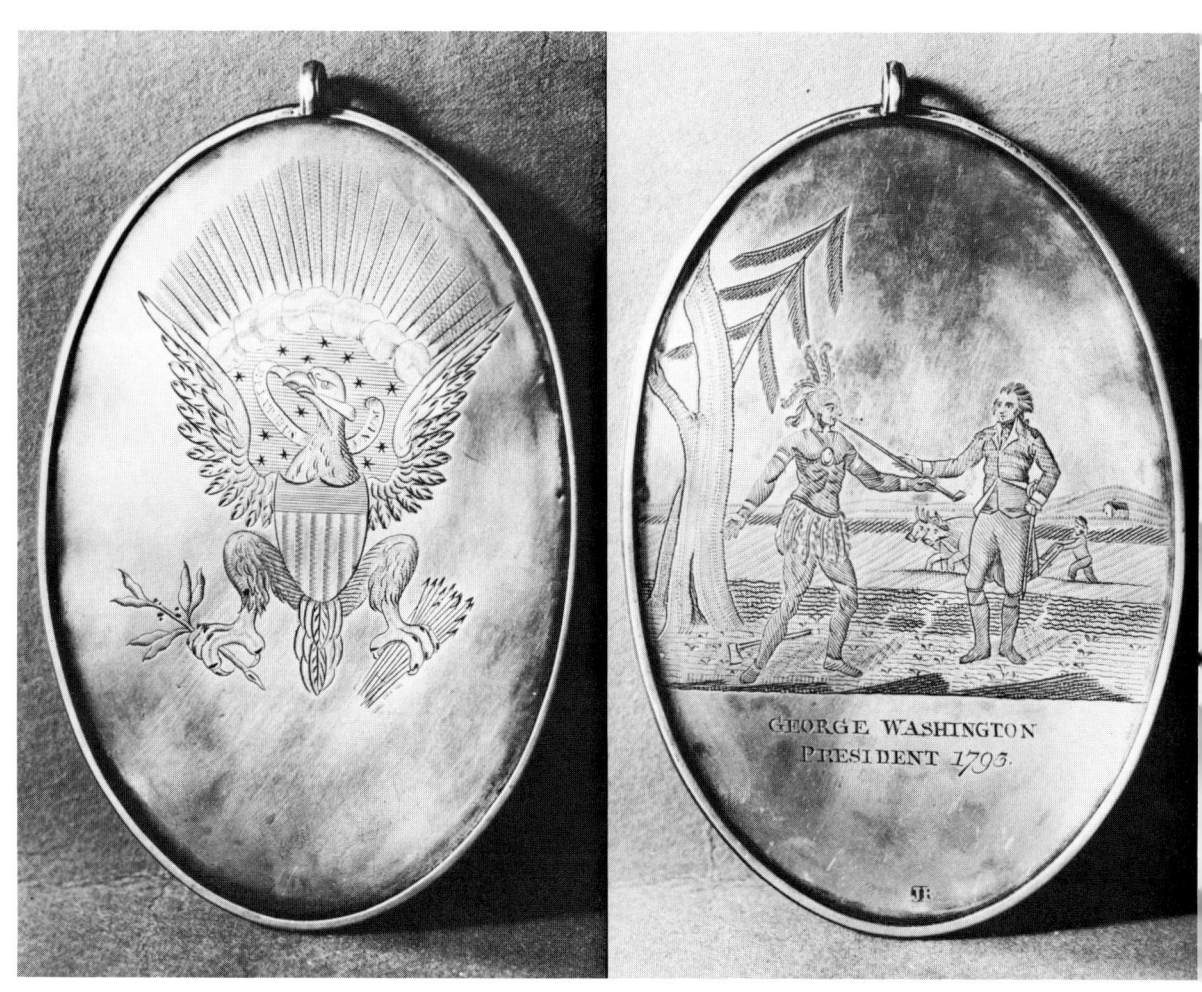

GEORGE WASHINGTON
PRESIDENT 1793.

*A medal engraved with an image of President George Washington
and an Indian. It was given to Wyandot chief Tarhee in 1793.*

THE

FORMATIVE YEARS
1777 TO 1815

Almost as soon as the French and Indian War ended, the victor, Great Britain, met opposition from its North American colonies. The crux of the disagreement was taxation: The British government held that it could tax the colonies without their consent. Another important issue was England's Indian policy. Because France had withdrawn its claim to the territory west of the Appalachian Mountains, many colonists believed this new area should be opened to white settlement. But the Proclamation Line still hemmed them in, and they took out their frustration on the mother country.

In 1776 the colonists declared their independence from Great Britain, and the American Revolution began. The colonists feared that the Indians would side with the British, and with good reason: It was the colonists who had taken over Indian territory and barged onto hallowed land. On the other hand, it was British officials who had stepped in to protect Indian land and furs from the colonists, and British traders who had brought the Indians valuable goods.

This history was well known to the Continental Congress, a group of delegates representing all of the colonies, which first convened in 1774. From the outset, the congress was anxious to find a way to ensure the Indians' neutrality. It formed a committee to recommend a course of action. On July 12, 1775, the committee announced its Indian policy. It called for the creation of three departments, each responsible for, in the words of the committee, "securing and preserving the friendship of the Indian nations." One department handled the Indians living in the North; another handled the South; a third handled those in the middle colonies. Each department was assigned from three to five commissioners, who were required to act "in the name, and on behalf of the united colonies."

But the colonists and the English underestimated the independence of some Indian groups. The English, for example, counted on the neutrality of the Cherokee, whose land, in what is now Tennessee, was shrinking under the steady advance of colonial settlers. But the Cherokee did not trust the English to protect their interests and instead took matters into their own hands by attacking two new settlements in 1776. Colonial governments in the South assumed that the English had put the Cherokee up to the attack and retaliated by setting fire to Cherokee villages. This was the first step in the decline of the Cherokee Nation, which lost half its territory following the American Revolution.

In the North, allegiances were more complex; sometimes they put Indians at odds with one another, as in the case of the Six Nations of the Iroquois, a confederacy founded in about 1570 by the Cayuga, Mohawk, Oneida, Onondaga, and Seneca, and joined by the Tuscarora in 1711. They claimed that their lands stretched far to the west, but they actually inhabited the area along the Hudson River in New York. When the American Revolution began, Mohawk chief Joseph Brant (also known as Thayendanegea) formed an alliance with the British. Other Iroquois tribes followed his example, but two, the Oneida and Tuscarora, sided with the Americans and were attacked for it by other members of the confederacy. Thus the powerful Iroquois confederation was split.

In 1781, as victory approached, the 13 independent states recognized that they must unite to form a central government that would outlast the war effort. The result was the first constitution of the United States—the Articles of Confederation. Because the colonists disliked the idea of a strong central government—such as England had—the Articles established a weak alliance that guaranteed each state its "sovereignty, freedom, and independence." However, they permitted a Confederation Congress to enact some national legislation and to speak for the interests of the states on foreign policy issues.

The Articles also shaped an Indian policy. They gave the central government the sole right to regulate trade and to manage affairs with the Indians in the unsettled areas that stretched from the Appalachian Mountains to the Mississippi River. This meant that as the United States extended its holdings, the central government would have the final say on all issues involving Indians. The Articles placated the 13 states by allowing each to retain the right to deal with the Indians within its borders as it alone saw fit.

In order to administer its Indian policy, the new government maintained the departments created by the Continental Congress, but in 1786 it streamlined them into a single Indian Department. Instead of three districts, there now were two. The northern district included all the Indian nations west of the Hudson River; the southern district included all those south of the Ohio River. A superintendent of Indian affairs, appointed by Congress, supervised each district and reported to the secretary of war.

Initially, the department supervised trade between Indians and settlers and mediated the disputes that often erupted. A serious issue was alcohol. White traders had discovered that many Indians had a low tolerance for liquor, which was new to many of them. Traders often tried to get Indians drunk and then trick them into giving up valuable pelts and skins. Some Indians became addicted to whiskey or rum and would swap high-quality goods for a few bottles of alcohol. In 1802, Congress authorized the president to regulate and even prohibit the sale of alcohol to Indians, for their own protection.

Another issue of concern to the Indian Department was land. In the 1780s, the Confederation government had begun to negotiate treaties with the Indians inhabiting the land closest to American settlements. These treaties reflected the popular belief that Americans had inherited title to all the lands formerly claimed by England between the Appalachians and the Mississippi River and that Indians in this area had no rights because they had been conquered. In the agreements, Indians were forced to cede land to the United States without compensation.

Mohawk chief Joseph Brant, who encouraged warriors from four Iroquois tribes to fight on the side of the British in the American Revolution.

The Indians, however, soon repudiated these treaties and turned to the English in Canada and the Spanish in Florida for support. It was readily given. Faced with the reality that the Indians could be forced to honor the treaties only through bloody and costly wars that the new states could ill afford, the Americans changed their policy.

In 1787 the Confederation Congress adopted the Northwest Ordinance, a series of laws that were to govern the Northwest Territory (the area of the

United States that was north of the Ohio River). The Congress now announced a policy of "utmost good faith" toward the Indians there. Indian lands and property would never be taken without their consent, Indians would be compensated for any lands they agreed to cede, and Indian lands would never again be invaded or disturbed "except in just and lawful wars authorized by Congress."

In truth, the United States was motivated not by fairness but by weakness and fear. The Revolution had taken its toll, and the struggling republic was not equipped to do battle with the western Indians. A wiser policy, therefore, was to purchase lands already overrun by settlers and patiently wait for the displaced Indians to move farther west. President George Washington, who took office in 1789, his secretary of war, Henry Knox, and other leaders believed that as white settlements and farms edged onto Indian country, wild game in the area would become scarce. The Indians, many of whom obtained much of their food by hunting, would then be willing to sell their lands cheaply and move west into remote areas Americans had not even begun to explore, let alone settle.

Washington and Knox counseled their fellow citizens to be mindful of the United States's "national honor." They urged that instead of exterminating the Indians, Amerians should recognize Indian ownership of the land they occupied and should pay them fair prices for it. Washington and Knox believed

Henry Knox. As secretary of war under President George Washington, Knox counseled Americans to respect the Indians' ownership of their homelands.

that in time the forces of Christianity and "superior" American culture would transform Indians into settled farmers who could become absorbed into mainstream society. This deluded belief would distort the nation's view of Indians long after events had proved it wrong.

By this time, the United States had replaced the Articles of Confederation with the Constitution, which called for a stronger federal government. The Constitution mentions the Indians only twice. Article I, Section 2 states that "Indians not taxed" would be excluded from the population count that determined the number of representatives each state would send to the Congress and the amount of tax owed by each state. This clause implied that Indians were not citizens of the United States. Article I, Section 8 (a carryover from the Articles of Confederation, called the "commerce clause") authorized Congress to "regulate Commerce with foreign nations, and among the several states, and with the Indian Tribes." Upon this slender legal base and the experience of the colonial powers that preceded it, the entire edifice of the United States's Indian policy has been built.

Beginning in 1790, Congress passed a series of laws to "regulate trade and intercourse" with the Indians and in 1796 recognized the lands west of the Proclamation Line as an Indian country, in which Indian rights were to be protected. Like England's Proclamation Line, the new laws allowed only the federal government—not states or private citizens—to negotiate for Indian lands. The federal government also regulated which Americans could enter Indian lands, and it assumed jurisdiction over major crimes, such as murder, that whites might commit against Indians in the Indian country. Traders were required to obtain government licenses and to post bonds that would be forfeited if they failed to observe the laws. Mindful of the harm caused by greedy and dishonest traders, the government subsidized its own trading posts, usually alongside military forts. After modifying the various trade and intercourse acts throughout the 1790s, Congress incorporated them into the Trade and Intercourse Act of 1802.

These laws were sometimes difficult to enforce in areas populated by pioneering Americans. The government often found it impossible to keep them off lands that they were intent on settling. Indians objected furiously to the intrusion of whites, who often tried simply to seize land. Government officials understood this. No one explained the problem more evenhandedly than Secretary of War Henry Knox. As he wrote in 1794:

> The desires of too many frontier white people, to seize, by force or fraud, upon the neighboring Indian lands has been, and still continues to be, an unceasing cause of jealousy and hatred on the part of the Indians; and it would appear, upon a calm investigation, that, until the Indians

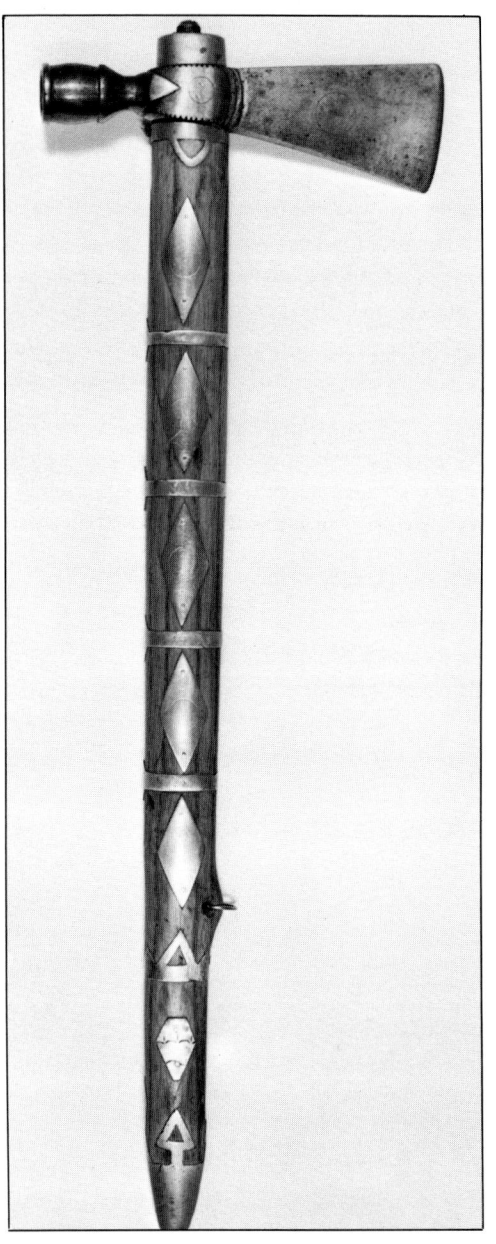

Decorated with silver, this pipe tomahawk was presented to Indian leader Little Turtle by General Anthony Wayne in 1795.

can be quieted upon this point, and rely with confidence upon the protection of their lands by the United States, no well grounded hope of tranquillity can be entertained.

Matters came to a head in 1790, when settlers pressed into the fertile lands north of the Ohio River, where Miami and Shawnee Indians lived. The settlers were not violating federal law: The land had been purchased by the United States in 1789 through the Treaty of Fort Harmar. Nevertheless the Indians resisted white settlement in their homeland. The Constitution obligated President Washington to protect the settlers. He was also intent upon demonstrating the strength of the new constitutional government. As a result, he ordered federal troops into what is now Ohio to force the Indians there to honor the treaty.

In 1790, General Hosiah Harmar set off with 1,400 troops to face a combined force of Shawnee, Miami, Potawatomi, and Chippewa. The Indians' commander, a Miami named Little Turtle, lured Harmar into the Maumee Valley and set fire to several Indian villages, usually a sign of flight. But this time it was a trick. Little Turtle had led the inexperienced troops into the dense woods, where they were poorly equipped to do battle. The Indian forces surrounded Harmar's soldiers and killed 183. More would have died had Little Turtle not allowed them to escape.

Although Harmar boasted that he had won, President Washington removed him from command and appointed in his place General Arthur St. Clair, the governor of the Northwest Territory. But he turned out to be no more competent an Indian fighter than Harmar. Heading an army composed mostly of amateur soldiers—600 of whom deserted when they did not receive the pay they had been promised—St. Clair set up his forces without bothering to build barricades or to post lookouts. Little Turtle sprang an early-morning attack, and St. Clair was routed.

In 1794, Washington turned to revolutionary war hero Major General Anthony Wayne, a brilliant soldier. Little Turtle recognized him as a formidable opponent and urged his fellow chiefs to settle peacefully. They rejected his advice and put their faith in Turkey Foot, who led an Indian force against Wayne in mid-August 1794 at a place called Fallen Timbers near present-day Toledo, Ohio. Wayne defeated them.

A year later, the tribes of the western Indian conspiracy were forced to sign the Treaty of Greenville. They ceded most of what is now central and southern Ohio and agreed that the United States had the right to "preempt," or purchase, the remainder of their lands north of the Ohio River and east of the Mississippi at some future date. Until this happened, the defeated Indians were forced to accept the presence of federal troops at 16 sites

General Anthony Wayne, who defeated the Indian force led by Turkey Foot at the Battle of Fallen Timbers in 1794.

linked by a connecting network of roads throughout the lands they still retained. Many tribes that inhabited this area were not represented at the signing of the Treaty of Greenville and therefore were not aware of these provisions.

In the same year, the United States successfully negotiated a treaty with Great Britain in which the English agreed to abandon their forts in the Northwest Territory and retreat to Canada. Thus by 1795 the United States not only had successfully demonstrated its military strength to the Indians in the area north of the Ohio River but deprived them of their most powerful ally.

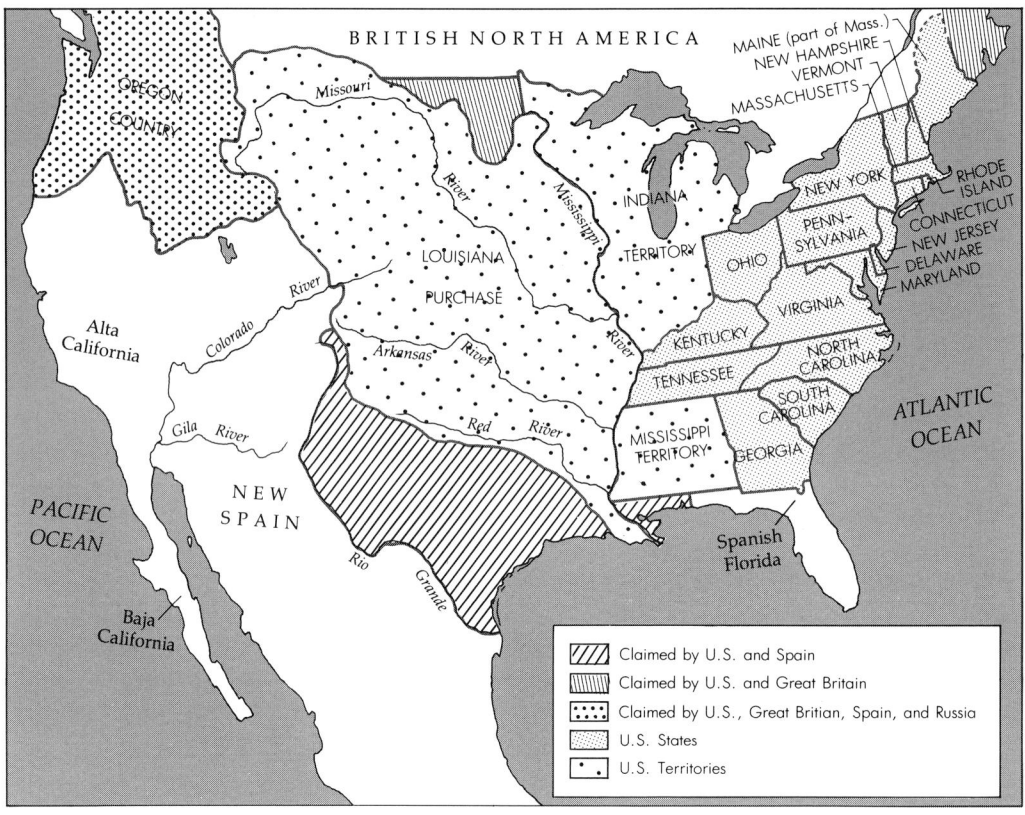

The U.S. Army bested the Indians at Fallen Timbers, but the number of its casualties was high. The federal government did not want to muster its meager forces and resources south of the Ohio River. This area was inhabited by powerful tribes, such as the Cherokee, Creek, Choctaw, and Chickasaw, who were often aided by the Spanish in present-day Florida and in the area west of the Mississippi, then known as Louisiana. American frontiersmen, stymied by the Indian presence, complained about the federal government's unwillingness to intercede on their behalf. Frustrated, they turned to the state governments and insisted they remove the Indians from their homelands. This created the potential for a clash between the state and federal governments for the control of Indian policy in the South.

The first president to cope with this growing problem in the West was Thomas Jefferson, who was elected in 1801. Jefferson encouraged the Indians living east of the Mississippi to move farther west. One form of encouragement was his decision, in 1803, to purchase Louisiana from France, which had obtained the area from Spain in 1800. Louisiana Territory was a vast tract of land: East to west, it stretched from the Mississippi River to the Rocky Mountains; north to south, it reached from the Gulf of Mexico to what is now Canada. In fact, Jefferson's acquisition doubled the size of the United States.

Just as important, the acquisition of Louisiana gave the United States control of the Mississippi River. This opened the way for white settlers who had long been clamoring for the land between the Mississippi and the Appalachians. To meet the demands of these white Americans, Jefferson sought to negotiate new treaties with the Indians in this area that would provide for their peaceful removal to Louisiana Territory. North of the Ohio River, Jefferson's policy was implemented by General William Henry Harrison, the governor of Indiana Territory (and later the ninth president of the United States). There, to some extent, Jefferson's plan worked.

South of the Ohio, Indians were more resistant. Jefferson himself persuaded some Cherokees to move to Arkansas Territory but, in general, Indian groups in the middle and southern United States saw no reason to give up their homes. Unlike the Indians north of the Ohio, they had not been defeated in battle. They were prosperous, settled farmers, and their numbers were large. One group, the Cherokee in Georgia,

even adopted many white customs. They sent their children to English-language schools, devised a Cherokee alphabet (so their language could be written as well as spoken), and built plantations that were farmed by black slaves. The Cherokee even drew up a constitution modeled on the American document. In the Cherokee constitution, these Indians asserted that they were citizens of an independent and sovereign nation with sole jurisdiction over their lands.

Jefferson and his immediate successors to the presidency refused to force Indians to remove to Louisiana Territory. Nevertheless, many Indians feared that the United States would eventually make them relocate to western lands. By 1810 the Indians of the Northwest Territory had begun to unite in an effort to retain their homelands. This confederacy was led by two Shawnees from present-day Ohio, Tenskwatawa (the Prophet) and his brother, Tecumseh.

The Prophet preached a powerful message. He argued that the Indians had become victims of whites because they had rejected their own traditional ways and had taken up the habits of their enemies. In order to regain their former strength, he insisted, Indians would have to abandon all the trappings of white society. The Prophet's brother, Tecumseh, added that the sale of their lands had degraded them and made them powerless. They could prevent the further advance of the whites

Sequoyah, the inventor of the Cherokee alphabet. The silver medal around his neck was given to him by the Cherokee legislature in 1824 to honor his achievement.

only by banding together and refusing to sell any more territory. After winning the support of many of the Indians in the Northwest Territory, Tecumseh began to add members of some southern Indian tribes to his confederation. General Harrison, alarmed at the growing Indian resistance, marched against the Prophet's followers in what is now Indiana in 1811. Losses on both sides were heavy in the ensuing Battle of Tippecanoe, but Harrison succeeded in burning the Prophet's town and scattering his followers.

The next year, hostilities broke out again between the United States and Great Britain. During this conflict, known as the War of 1812, many of the Indians in the Northwest teamed up with the British in attacks upon American settlements. They overran American forts near what are now Detroit, Michigan, and Chicago, Illinois. Then, in October 1813, Harrison attacked the British and their Indian allies in Canada and defeated them in the Battle of the Thames. Tecumseh died in this battle. Without his leadership and without British support, the Indians of the Northwest became dispirited and disorganized.

Earlier, on a journey south to encourage the Indians there to join his confederation, Tecumseh had rallied some young Creek warriors to his cause. Buoyed by Tecumseh's false promise of British and Spanish assistance, they destroyed an American settlement near what is now Mobile, Alabama, in August 1813. In 1814 a force of American frontiersmen, led by a general of the Tennessee militia named Andrew Jackson, responded by attacking the Creek in the center of their territory at a place known as Horseshoe Bend. The Creek were soundly beaten and then forced to sign a treaty that deprived them of the eastern half of what is now Alabama.

As a result of the decisive military victories over the Indians during the War of 1812, the balance of power east of the Mississippi River shifted to the Americans. Treaties forced upon the vanquished northern tribes required them to abandon their homes and move westward into Louisiana

An 1833 lithograph of the death of Indian leader Tecumseh at the Battle of the Thames in 1813.

Territory, and settlers poured by the thousands onto the former Indian lands. South of the Ohio River, however, the Cherokee, Creek, Chickasaw, and Choctaw Indians looked to the federal government for protection. Arguing that the United States was obligated to honor earlier treaties that recognized their ownership of their lands, they refused to sign new treaties or to move west of the Mississippi River. The day would soon come, however, when Indians would be given little say in the matter. ▲

Trail of Tears, *a 1957 painting by Pawnee Indian Brumett Echo-
hawk, depicts the removal of the Cherokee to Indian Territory (now
Oklahoma) in the 1830s.*

INDIAN REMOVAL
1816 TO 1860

After the War of 1812, thousands of American pioneers rushed to stake out the territory between the original colonies and the Mississippi River. As the settlers arrived, the Indians were forced west; between 1816 and 1840, various tribes there signed more than 40 treaties that ceded land to the United States. Yet the major Indian nations south of the Ohio River—the Cherokee, Choctaw, Creek, Chickasaw, and Seminole—managed to stay put until the 1830s. Their decision to accept "removal," as the official policy was called, came only as the result of several developments. Perhaps the most important was Andrew Jackson's election to the presidency in 1828.

Jackson was born in 1767 in Waxhaw Settlement, on the border of North and South Carolina, but he moved to Tennessee in his youth and made his name there. He helped draft the state's con-

stitution and in 1796 was chosen to represent Tennessee in Congress. Jackson first became a major public figure in 1814 when he defeated the Creek at the Battle of Horseshoe Bend. Later, during the end of the War of 1812, he became a national hero when he defeated the British in 1815 at the Battle of New Orleans. After the war, Jackson was placed in charge of the U.S. Army in the Southwest. He blundered badly, however, in 1818, when he went after Seminole Indians who had left Spanish Florida to raid American settlements in Alabama and Georgia. Jackson pursued them into Florida, a clear violation of international law that greatly embarrassed the U.S. government. Jackson barely escaped court-martial.

The incident reaped unexpected rewards, though, for both Jackson and the United States. His spree exposed the weakness of Spain's control in Flor-

President Andrew Jackson, who pushed Congress to pass legislation that would require eastern Indians to relocate west of the Mississippi.

ida and thereby enabled the United States to negotiate a treaty that wrested Florida from the Spanish in 1819. This treaty removed the last foreign threat to American expansion east of the Mississippi River.

To whites on the frontier, where animosity toward Indians was great, Jackson became a legend. He lacked the polish of educated statesmen like John Adams and Thomas Jefferson, but he embodied the proud regional spirit growing on the frontier, where citizens hungered to play a role in shaping the political destiny of the nation. In 1824,

Jackson ran for president but lost a tight race to John Quincy Adams of Massachusetts. In 1828, Jackson ran again— and won.

Jackson was a vocal proponent of American expansionism. He believed it would be impossible for the United States to become a strong nation if it permitted the Indians to remain independent of its authority. Instead, he argued, Indians should become citizens of the state or territory in which they resided and be accorded the same rights and responsibilities as other citizens. If they refused, they should be forced to move farther west, beyond the Mississippi, where they would not impede the development of the United States.

Jackson's belief in removal was shared by many self-styled friends of the Indians. These reformers were alarmed by the dismal history of relations between Indians and whites. They noted that whenever the two came into contact the Indians suffered woefully. They lost their land, were lured into alcoholism, and became a general threat and nuisance to themselves and to their neighbors. The only hope of "saving" the Indians was to get them away from the advancing frontiersmen who had brought them such misery.

This point of view became official policy in 1829, when, in his first address to Congress, Jackson called for federal legislation that would require eastern Indians to remove to areas west of the Mississippi River. Congress debated the plan at length and officially adopted it in 1830.

Even before passage of the Indian Removal Act, trouble was brewing between the federal government and the state of Georgia over the status of the Cherokee Indians. Some 30 years earlier, during the administration of President Jefferson, the government assured the state of Georgia that it would persuade the Cherokee to give up land promised them by a previous treaty. As the years wore on, the federal government had tried to evict the Cherokee, but the Indians knew their rights and insisted the land was theirs. In 1828 the Georgia legislature, incensed by the federal government's inaction, took matters into its own hands and enacted a law extending the authority of the state over the Cherokee lands. The Cherokee were given an ultimatum: Accept this authority or move. Shortly after Jackson became president, Mississippi gave a similar one to the Choctaw who lived within its boundaries.

In 1830 the Cherokee hired several prominent lawyers and went to court to protect their land claims. The first of two Supreme Court decisions, *Cherokee Nation v. Georgia* (1831), stated that the Cherokee were "domestic, dependent nations" subject to the ultimate authority of the federal government. This defeat contained the seeds of victory, however. If the Indians were "domestic, dependent nations," they could not be ordered around as easily as the state of Georgia wished. This was confirmed in a second case, *Worcester v. Georgia* (1832). The Indians lost their claim to independent nation status, but they received assurance that they would not be subjected to state laws.

Neither the Cherokee nor the Supreme Court, however, reckoned on the determination of Andrew Jackson, who ignored these rulings. When the Georgia state government continued to force the Cherokee to obey its laws, President Jackson did nothing to prevent it. Instead, he pressured Indian leaders to sign a new treaty that provided for their removal to Indian country. By this time Jackson had successfully forced new treaties on the Choctaw, Creek, Chickasaw, and Seminole. The Cherokee finally succumbed as well, but only because Jackson approved a treaty that had been signed by just one small faction of the Cherokee people. In fact, all these treaties were tainted: Some were obtained through bribery; others through threats and intimidation.

The Indians well knew they were being strong-armed, and some would not budge when the time came for removal. Jackson then sent in the U.S. Army. The Seminole retreated into the swampy everglades of Florida. Many went to war with the U.S. Army and resisted deportation until their final defeat in 1842. Many others were never discovered. (In 1911, their descendants were finally given a small area of land in southern Florida. Today, a Seminole reservation is located there.)

Under the terms of the removal treaties, the southern Indians could remain on their lands if they renounced their allegiance to their respective tribe and accepted the authority of the state in which they lived. In practice, however, whites refused to recognize Indian ownership of land, and the federal government did nothing to protect it. Some Indians migrated westward to join their people, but others retreated to remote areas where they eked out a meager living on land that eventually was sold to whites. Thus, they became landless and homeless wanderers, without political or economic rights.

For those southern Indians who did remove, the westward trek to their new home was often brutal. Government officials proved stingy in allocating funds. Often they washed their hands of the arrangement and contracted with local whites to manage the removal. The results were disastrous. An estimated 4,000 Cherokees died on their Trail of Tears to the present state of Oklahoma. When the Creek resisted their eviction from Alabama, many were transported by the U.S. Army in chains. Some estimates put the death toll of Creeks killed in Alabama and on their westward journey at 3,500.

The government had no plan for receiving these uprooted Indians once they reached Indian country. This vast land was already inhabited by other Indian groups that reacted violently to the sudden influx of new arrivals. The new Indians and the white traders also brought diseases that severely reduced

Seminole leader Osceola at the 1834 negotiations for the removal of his people from present-day Florida. At this meeting, Osceola angrily plunged a knife into the removal treaty, which he refused to sign.

the Indian populations already living there.

As removal continued, the federal government found it necessary to upgrade its management of Indian affairs. The process was complicated by a step taken in 1824, when Secretary of War John C. Calhoun reorganized the Indian Department into a new federal agency, the Bureau of Indian Affairs (BIA), without bothering to secure the approval of Congress. The BIA's staff was on the payroll of the War Department, which also determined its budget and had to approve every act undertaken by its director, from settling land claims to signing off on correspondence.

The bureaucratic tangle was partly unknotted in 1832, when Congress gave the agency's director a new title, commissioner of Indian affairs, and granted him the power to act more independently. Congress in 1834 made the agency completely independent of the War Department and directly accountable to Congress. This happened in time for the BIA, under Commissioner Elbert Herring, to carry out Andrew Jackson's removal policy.

Also in 1834, Congress passed a new Trade and Intercourse Act, updating previous laws. The United States again delineated an Indian country and made it off limits to all whites except those who received special authorization. The designated area, which later became known as Indian Territory, included all the land west of the Mississippi River except for Arkansas Territory, Louisi-

ana, and Missouri. Penalties against trespassers were stiffened, but there were not enough local BIA employees, or agents, to enforce them.

Between 1830 and 1850 about 100,000 Indians were moved into an area usually referred to as the "permanent Indian country." The plan was for the Indians to continue their traditions of hunting and farming until they absorbed the customs of white civilization. They could then apply for admittance of the territory into the Union. More immediately, the Indian country served as a buffer between American settlers and British and Spanish colonists who laid claim to territory beyond the Rocky Mountains. The U.S. government left the Indians alone; interference came only when the army occasionally tried to make peace between rival Indian groups.

This quiet interlude was rudely shattered in 1846 when the United States set about to achieve what would later be called its manifest destiny—the extension of its western border to the Pacific Ocean. This policy partly originated in the belief commonly held by Americans—and inherited from their European predecessors—that they belonged to a privileged culture, one that could only bring good wherever it was introduced. There was also a practical consideration. American settlers were filling up the territory east of the Mississippi and wanted to press on farther, into the Oregon country (claimed jointly by the United States and England) and into the sparsely settled re-

(continued on page 44)

REMOVAL AND THE CHEROKEE INDIANS

American Indians have been losing their lands to non-Indians since the first Europeans settled in North America in the 16th century. Initially, these settlers were content to share land with the Indians. As the non-Indians' population grew, however, they began to overrun tribes' traditional homelands. When, by the beginning of the 19th century, unoccupied fertile land had become scarce in the East, American settlers clamored for the government to forcibly remove Indians from their territory.

President Thomas Jefferson first proposed that eastern Indians be relocated west of the Mississippi River during the early 1800s, but it was not until the presidency of Andrew Jackson (1829–37) that tribes were faced with forced removal. Under pressure from non-Indian politicians, the U.S. Congress passed the Indian Removal Act of 1830, which authorized President Jackson to negotiate land sales with such powerful southeastern tribes as the Cherokee, Choctaw, and Chickasaw. Representatives of the president soon met with these tribes' leaders to discuss the terms of treaties that would provide for the sale of the Indians' homelands, the purchase of new lands for them in Indian Territory (originally portions of present-day Kansas, Nebraska, and Oklahoma), and the Indians' removal there. The U.S. officials often bribed or intimidated these leaders to persuade them to sign treaties that were not advantageous to their people. Although the agreements were considered valid and legally binding by the United States, few Indians felt that the government's representatives had dealt with them honorably or even honestly.

The Cherokee were particularly embittered by the government's conduct. They consequently engaged in a series of futile legal battles to retain their homeland but were eventually compelled to negotiate with the United States. In December 1835, U.S. treaty commissioners purposely sought out a minority group of Cherokee (about 100) who were known to favor removal and, with their consent, drafted the Treaty of New Echota. The treaty provided for the exchange of all Cherokee lands in the Southeast for a parcel of land in what is now northeastern Oklahoma. Fifteen thousand Cherokees signed a petition protesting the treaty, but the U.S. government ignored it and ratified the agreement anyway.

The Cherokee were given two years to prepare for their journey to Indian Territory. But, confident that the government would come to its senses and rescind its unjust treaty, the Cherokee made no plans for removal. In the summer of 1838, frustrated by the Indians' inaction, the government sent federal troops to Cherokee territory to begin rounding up the Indians and imprisoning them in stockades.

The Trail of Tears, *painted by Robert Lindneux in 1840. Thousands of Cherokee died during the arduous journey westward.*

While the U.S. government was forming its plan for Cherokee removal, the Indians at the prison camps suffered greatly from inadequate supplies of food and water. In desperation, Cherokee chief John Ross, who vehemently opposed removal, and other tribal leaders appealed to President Martin Van Buren to allow the Cherokee to make their own arrangements for their march westward. The president approved the plan and, in the winter of 1838–39, the Cherokee began the long trek to their new home.

The journey proved a deadly blow to the Cherokee people. Between one-fourth and one-half of the tribe died of exhaustion, starvation, and exposure during the long trip. U.S. Army private John G. Burnett, who participated in the Cherokee removal, wrote, "The long painful journey to the west ended March 26, 1839, with four thousand silent graves. . . . And the covetousness . . . of the white race was the cause." The Cherokee tribe, more than many others, had tried to accommodate the demands of the U.S. government. Their disastrous removal, now known as the Trail of Tears, was their reward.

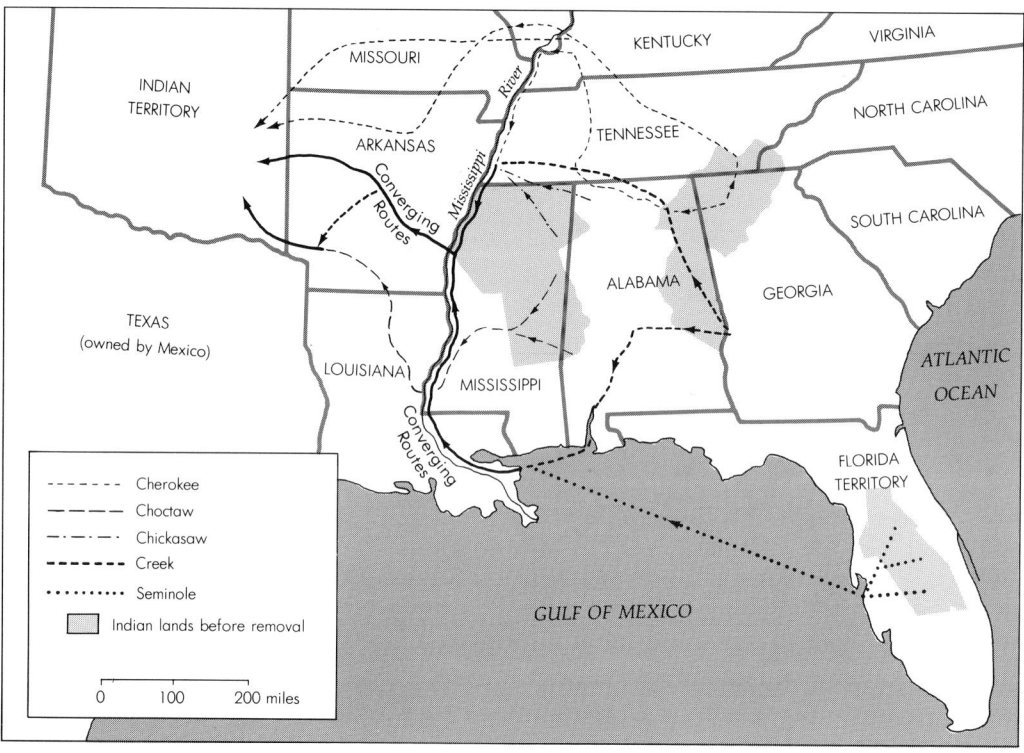

(continued from page 41)

gion stretching from what is now Texas to California (claimed by Mexico).

In 1846 the United States took steps to secure both regions. A treaty with Great Britain, backed by the threat of war, put the Oregon Territory squarely in American hands. During the Mexican War, which lasted until 1848, the United States wrested two-fifths of Mexico's land holdings. These additions gave the growing nation control of a huge territory—almost all of what now constitutes the American Southwest. The result was that the Indian Territory, earlier considered a permanent buffer between the United States and its rivals to the west, now became squeezed between two populations of Americans.

Problems had already surfaced in Indian Territory. Even before the Mexican War, white pioneers began to interfere with the Indians there. Some passed through on their way to the Oregon Territory or to Utah Territory, where a religious sect, the Church of Jesus Christ of Latter-day Saints (commonly called the Mormons) was founding settlements. Still others followed a southern route along the Santa Fe Trail to Mexican lands. Many of these migrants hunted buffalo—the prime source of food and clothing for many Indians—destroyed pastures and scarce timber stands, and brought diseases that devastated Indian populations that had no immunity to them.

Throughout the West, tension mounted between the Indians and the whites. Whites encroached on Indian hunting lands; Indians answered by attacking wagon trains. The federal government responded by building forts in Indian Territory.

Meanwhile, the United States government faced a new question: how best to unite its new western holdings with the rest of the nation. The question could have been left to simmer for some time, considering how few Americans had actually put down roots in the new territories. But in 1849 the discovery of gold in present-day California lured thousands of prospectors into the area and forced the issue. The government decided a railroad was the quickest and most efficient means for joining the East and the West. But the question remained as to what route it should take. Building and operating a railroad could be enormously profitable, and every congressman wanted his voters to benefit. Southern legislators proposed that the railroad run between California and Memphis, Tennessee, or New Orleans, Louisiana. Northerners favored a route that ran through Chicago, Illinois.

A much larger issue lay behind this regional squabble: slavery. The nation was sharply divided between states that permitted slavery and those that outlawed it. The official policy of the federal government was tolerance: States with slaves could keep them. Many northerners, however, called for an end to slavery throughout the Union. For the time being, the southern states were strongly enough represented in Congress to hold their opponents at bay, but they feared that the addition of new territories, which would soon apply for statehood, could tilt the existing balance between proslavery and antislavery forces. As settlers and prospectors began to populate the West, the conflict between North and South intensified.

The two sides compromised in 1854. The railroad would run through Chicago, as the northerners wished. In return, the southerners were promised that two new territories, Kansas and Nebraska, would be created from the northern half of Indian Territory. White settlers, including slave owners, would then be free to move there. This potentially enlarged the number of slave states in the Union. It also superseded an earlier bill, the Missouri Compromise, passed in 1820–21, which banned slavery from most of the land acquired in the Louisiana Purchase. The Kansas-Nebraska Act, as the 1854 legislation was called, touched off a debate that would eventually lead to the Civil War.

Few debaters noted that the compromise violated the rights of Indians living in the "permanent" Indian country. Anticipating a rapid influx of whites into Kansas and Nebraska territories, the BIA quickly began to negotiate a series of treaties with the Indians living there. Following a pattern it had adopted previously in California and in the Oregon and Washington territories, the BIA persuaded Indians to cede tracts large enough to form a corridor through which wagon trains and the railroad could run. In return, those Indians who wished to live alongside whites received land allotments—individually owned plots of land—and those who wanted to retain their traditional way of life were granted reservations, areas set aside for occupation and use by Indians only. In the end, it mattered little what the Indians chose. Most of those who received allotments were chased off them by invading whites, and some reservations in Kansas Territory were also overrun.

While the federal government was opening the Kansas and Nebraska territories to white settlement, it also began negotiations with powerful Plains Indian peoples, including the Cheyenne and Comanche, who lived north and south of the Kansas-Nebraska corridor. The BIA respected the war-making ability of these nations and made no attempt to confine them to reservations at this time. The bureau instead obtained their permission to establish military posts and trails in this area in return for specified gifts or annuities.

Typical of these treaties was one signed in 1855 by representatives of the Blackfoot Nation, who lived near the upper Missouri River in the Nebraska Territory. The government promised to pay "in addition to the goods and pro-

A drawing sent by the Osage Indians to the federal government in the mid-1800s as a protest against the construction of a railroad across their land in Kansas Territory.

visions distributed at the time of signing this treaty, twenty thousand dollars, annually for ten years. . . . *Provided, however,* That if, in the judgment of the President and Senate, this amount be deemed insufficient, it may be increased not to exceed the sum of thirty-five thousand dollars per year." In return, the Blackfoot Nation, composed of the Blackfoot, Piegan, Blood, and Hidatsa Indians, agreed to establish no permanent settlements, to let American citizens "live in and pass unmolested through [their] countries," and to allow the United States to "construct roads of every description; establish lines of telegraph and military posts; use materials of every description found in the Indian country; build houses for agencies, missions, schools, farms, shops, mills, stations, and for any other purpose for which they may be required; and permanently occupy as much land as may be necessary."

The treaty, in sum, allowed the Indians to live on their own land but licensed the United States to lay the groundwork for prolonged settlement. Treaties with some other Indian groups at this time spelled out harsher terms. Farther north, the Sioux Indians signed a treaty ceding their lands in Minnesota and Iowa, except for a small reservation along the Mississippi River.

By the late 1850s, many Indian nations smoldered with resentment. Things came to a head during the Colorado gold rush of 1858. Over the next two years, miners surged across the Rocky Mountains and then into Indian

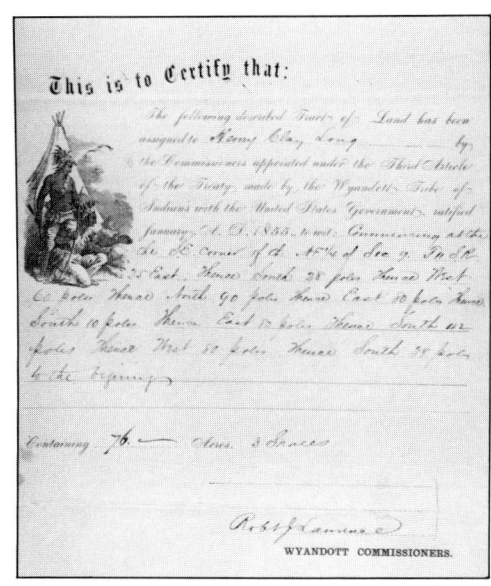

A deed that granted a plot of land in Kansas Territory to a Wyandot Indian in 1855. The Bureau of Indian Affairs gave Indians in Kansas and Nebraska territories the option of living on their own land allotments alongside whites or of staying within the boundaries of a reservation.

lands in what are now Idaho and Montana. When Indians attacked the prospectors, the U.S. Army stepped in. In 1861 the Civil War began, and the federal government suddenly recalled many of these troops. Some Indian nations—the Sioux, Cheyenne, and Arapaho to the north; the Navajo and Apache to the south—took advantage of this opportunity to drive the remaining whites out of their territory. Throughout the 1860s and 1870s a series of Indian wars raged across the West, and a new chapter in federal Indian policy began. ▲

A drawing by Lone Bear, an Oglala Sioux, of the U.S. Army's capture of Cheyenne chief Dull Knife during his band's attempt to flee from Indian Territory in 1878. The Sioux were trying to escape from officers there, who had withheld food, fuel, and water from the Indians in order to bully them into submission.

THE CIVIL WAR
AND
RESERVATION POLICY
1861 TO 1887

After the withdrawal of federal troops from the West in 1861, the conflict between whites and Indians in the region grew even uglier. Settlers, deprived of official protection, organized their own makeshift armies. These were often led by zealots bent on removing Indians by any means. The resulting atrocities, committed by whites and Indians alike, equaled those committed during the French and Indian War.

A major trouble spot was the land the United States acquired from Mexico, especially present-day New Mexico and Arizona. The U.S. Army maintained forts there, but it was forced to abandon them when the Civil War began. This freed Mescalero Apache and Navajo Indians to raid herds of horses and cattle owned by whites. The settlers fought back and there was bloodshed.

Soon the Civil War spilled into the West. Both sides tried to coax pioneers to join their forces, and battles raged across the desert and the Plains. In 1862, California troops established Northern (or Union) control over what is now Arizona, and a New Mexico Territory militia repulsed a Confederate army from Texas. Soon the California and New Mexico Territory militiamen were reorganized under the leadership of Brigadier General James H. Carleton and sent to fight the Mescalero Apache and the Navajo.

In 1862, Carleton developed a plan for expelling tribes from their homelands and forcing them onto reservations. There, he reasoned, they could subsist by farming and be restrained by a small number of troops. Congress approved, and that same year Carleton, aided by scout Kit Carson, forced about 500 Mescaleros to move to Bosque Redondo (Spanish for Round Grove) on

Brigadier General James H. Carleton, who masterminded the removal of the Navajo to Bosque Redondo in eastern New Mexico Territory in 1862.

the Pecos River in eastern New Mexico Territory. The Navajo, however, were more difficult to bully. A large nation, spread out over rugged terrain, they evaded U.S. troops for three years, even after Carson and his forces destroyed their crops and captured their livestock. These actions gradually wore the Navajo down, however, and, finally, facing starvation, some 8,300 surrendered. As many as 4,000 others escaped by fleeing to the south and west of their original territory.

General Carleton now had succeeded in relocating the Indians onto the Bosque Redondo reservation. But his problems—and the Indians'—were not solved. The general had planned less shrewdly than he thought. He had not studied the reservation's climate or

terrain, and neither was conducive to farming. The Mescalero and the Navajo willingly planted crops, but drought and insects destroyed them. Worse, the water in the Pecos River proved unhealthy.

The Indians could survive only by hunting, which meant they had to be permitted to leave the reservation. Some hunting parties never came back. Because of the crop failures, the U.S. government was forced to spend large sums of money on food for the Indians who remained on the reservation. By 1868, it was clear Carleton's experiment had failed. The Mescalero and the Navajo signed new treaties that allowed them to return to their homelands—or, rather, to the portion of their homelands that the federal government grudgingly returned.

The government's efforts to manage Indians to the north fared no better. A notorious example involved the Santee Sioux, who had been confined to small reservations in southern Minnesota Territory. In 1862, after poor harvests had left many Sioux on the brink of starvation, they became enraged when the government delayed annuity payments due them by the terms of an earlier treaty. The Sioux stormed the headquarters of the Indian agency and attacked nearby towns. They killed more than 400 settlers and captured an even larger number before being defeated by the federal troops that were quickly dispatched to the area. Hysterical settlers demanded the heads of the captured Sioux, who were hastily tried in military courts. Three hundred three Sioux were sentenced to death. President Abraham Lincoln intervened, but not before 38 Sioux were hanged in a public spectacle widely reported across the nation.

Even bloodier conflicts erupted near the Rockies. In Colorado, droves of settlers and miners traveled along the overland stage lines that led to Denver. The traffic disrupted the migration of the buffalo herds that were essential to the survival of the Cheyenne and Arapaho. Horsemen and warriors from these tribes began to attack wagon trains. When a group of Arapahos killed a white family in Denver, settlers demanded revenge—and got it in the person of Colonel John M. Chivington, who headed Colorado's military forces.

The first taste of vengeance came when Chivington sent troops to north-

ern Colorado, where they attacked several Cheyenne camps. Then, on May 16, 1864, troops met a large band of Cheyenne on a buffalo hunt in western Kansas. Their leader, Chief Lean Bear, had just returned from an audience with President Lincoln, who gave him a peace medal that gleamed brightly on Lean Bear's chest. The chief also carried a note, signed by Lincoln, that attested to his trustworthiness. None of this mattered to the troops, who shot him dead. In retaliation the Dog Soldiers, the Cheyenne's celebrated warrior corps, destroyed wagon trains and settlements.

Both sides had reached the breaking point. Colorado's territorial governor, John Evans, directed all friendly Indians to appear at the various government forts in the territory. Two

Navajo Indians constructing Fort Sumner under the guard of U.S. soldiers at the Bosque Redondo reservation in the mid-1860s.

important Cheyenne chiefs, Black Kettle and White Antelope, headed a peace delegation that met with Evans in Denver. Black Kettle made a speech, which was later repeated by the secretary of war on the floor of Congress: "We have come with our eyes shut, following a handful of men [U.S. Army troops], like coming through fire. All we ask is that we may have peace with the whites."

Eloquence went only so far. Evans was locked in a political fight with Colonel Chivington, and the voters wanted the Cheyenne dealt with one way or another. Evans denounced Black Kettle and White Antelope and blamed them for all the hostilities. His political rival Chivington took a more reasonable tone. When the peace conference ended, he told the chiefs: "My rule of fighting white men or Indians is, to fight them until they put down their arms and submit to military authority." He added that when the chiefs were ready to surrender, they should appear at Fort Lyon, Colorado.

On November 9, 1864, nine Cheyennes appeared at the fort. They reported that 600 of their people were en route, with 2,000 more to follow. The first 600 arrived and set up 113 lodges on the premises. They were destitute, but Fort Lyon's commander, Major Scott J. Anthony, would give them no food. He ordered Black Kettle's band, which was camped at Sand Creek, to stay put, under the protection of Anthony's troops.

What no one knew was that Governor Evans and Colonel Chivington were both under pressure. Voters wanted action. In August, Evans had outfitted a new regiment of volunteer cavalry, the Colorado Third, but it had yet to fire a round and its 100-day enlistment would end soon. The regiment had acquired a mocking nickname: the Bloodless Third. Chivington, who commanded the regiment, was embarrassed further by the sudden arrival in Denver of General P. E. Connor, a noted Indian-fighter.

Chivington responded by ordering the Bloodless Third to march toward Sand Creek and Black Kettle's encampment. On the way, Chivington stopped at Fort Lyon and added its troops to his forces, which now numbered 700, all heavily armed. He also brought along four large cannons. The army headed for Sand Creek.

They arrived at dawn. Black Kettle and his followers—men, women, and children—slept in tipis huddled near a bend in the Sand Creek River. Camp dogs barked at the sight of the troops, and Chivington ordered his troops to fire. Black Kettle raised an American flag, and White Antelope walked toward the soldiers unarmed, begging the troops not to shoot. Both were ignored. The soldiers murdered some 150 men, women, and children and then mutilated the bodies in an orgy of violence. White Antelope was killed, but Black Kettle escaped. Chivington later boasted that the Indian death count totaled between 400 and 500. Another soldier, General Nelson Miles, called the slaughter the "foulest and most unjus-

The public execution of 38 Santee Sioux following the tribe's uprising in Minnesota Territory in 1862. The Indians had killed more than 400 white settlers after a delay in the government's annuity payments left them starving.

tifiable crime in the annals of America.'' Chivington displayed his personal collection of Indian scalps, 100 in all, at a Denver theater.

The Navajo, Mescalero Apache, Sioux, Cheyenne, and Arapaho were all defeated. But Indians in the southern regions of Indian Territory initially escaped this fate. By the 1860s the Creek, Cherokee, Chickasaw, Choctaw, and Seminole—sometimes called the Five Civilized Tribes because they adopted many elements of white society—had established fairly prosperous nations in the West. The Civil War, however, threatened their independence. They were bordered on the east and south by states that had seceded from the Union to join the Confederacy, and all the U.S. Army troops in the area were recalled

to fight in the East. This left them relatively unprotected if the Confederate army or hostile settlers chose to invade their lands.

Even the tribes that favored the North felt they had no choice but to join forces with the South. But there were other reasons aside from fear of attack that made an alliance with the Confederacy attractive to the Five Civilized Tribes. Many of their leaders owned black slaves and consequently had strong sympathy for the South's position. Moreover, the Confederacy offered them greater freedom and more rights than they had received in treaties with the United States. For instance, they were promised the right of self-government, were guaranteed they would never be absorbed into any fu-

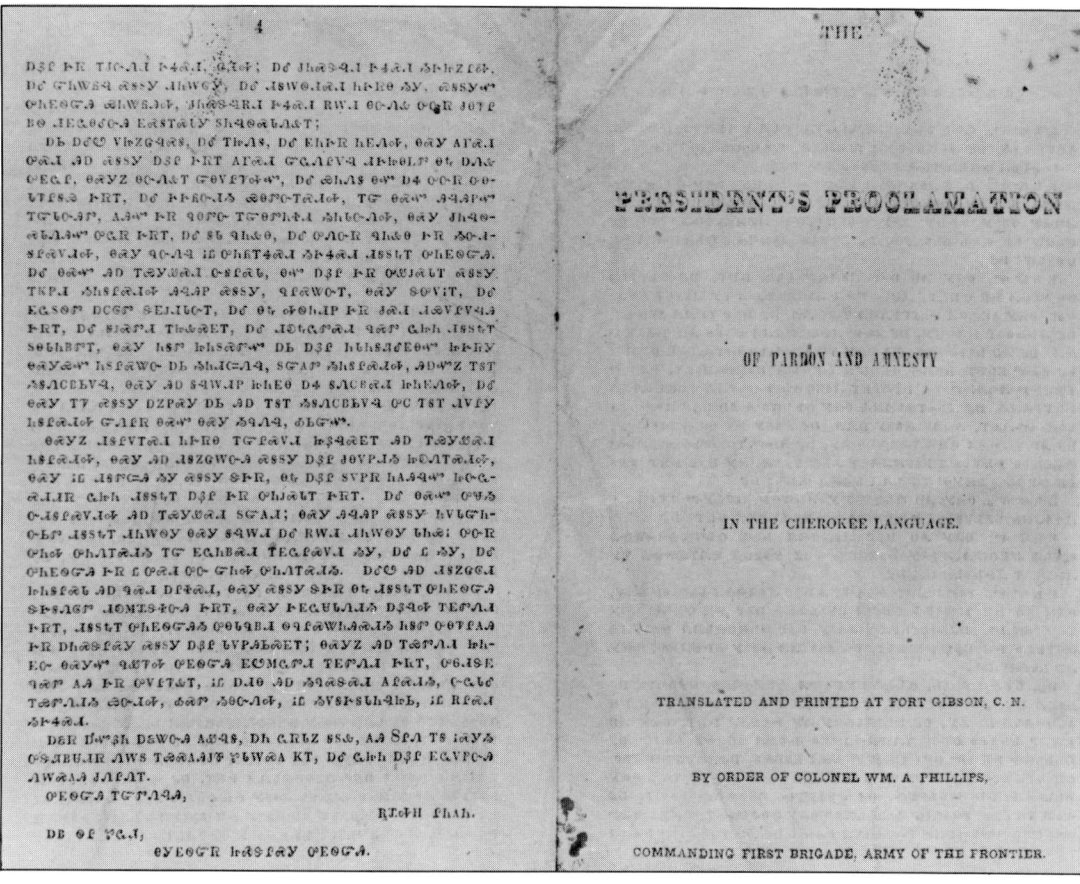

A Cherokee-language translation of President Abraham Lincoln's pardon and offer of amnesty to the Indians who had fought with the Confederate army during the Civil War.

ture state or territory and, in the case of the Cherokee, were even promised a seat in the Confederate legislature if they agreed to renounce the authority of the United States and join with the Confederacy.

These were powerful enticements, and the Choctaw, Chickasaw, Cherokee, and Creek signed treaties with the Confederacy. Many Cherokee and Creek Indians counseled neutrality, however, because they feared retaliation from the North if the South lost the war. These Indians fled north to Kansas, where they lived out the war in destitution. Those who stayed behind formed military units to defend Indian Territory, but the Indians, like the rest of the country, were divided into Confederate and Union factions and fought one another. When federal troops returned, the Confederacy provided little protection. Eventually the Indian military units were crushed.

Because the Five Civilized Tribes had formally allied with the South, they were punished, just as some of their leaders had predicted, when the war ended in 1865 and the North was victorious. They were forced to cede the western half of their lands to the federal government, which intended to settle other tribes there. Ironically, the Cherokee and the Creek, which had the largest number of pro-Union and neutral members, received the worst treatment in the treaties signed after the war.

Following the Civil War, the many conflicts in the West led the federal government to reevaluate its Indian policy. The first investigation was undertaken by a congressional committee headed by Senator James R. Doolittle in 1865. The committee submitted a report two years later that cited widespread fraud and corruption in the BIA and blamed most of the violence in the Plains on aggressive whites who encroached upon Indians' lands and destroyed the buffalo herds on which the Indians depended for survival. The Doolittle committee concluded that the Indians were now so weakened and vulnerable that there was no longer any recourse but to place them all on reservations, where they could be protected from the whites. Eventually, this advice would be followed.

A more immediate concern of the government was that some Teton Sioux were staging attacks on whites in the western Rockies, in what is now Mon-

An 1887 photograph of a Sioux woman and the members of the Indian Peace Commission. The commission was created by Congress in 1867 to help end warfare on the Plains.

tana. In 1865 a band led by Red Cloud kept miners off their hunting grounds near the Powder River by seizing army posts along the Bozeman Trail, a well-traveled route through present-day Wyoming and southern Montana. Congress wanted to negotiate treaties that would restore peace on the frontier

Sioux chief Red Cloud addressing an audience of whites at the Cooper Institute in New York City about the wrongs the government had committed against his people. This event was part of the chief's 1870 tour of the East, which was sponsored by the Indian Peace Commission.

and, at the same time, guarantee protection to the Indians.

To help in this effort, Congress created the United States Indian Peace Commission in 1867. It was made up of Christian reformers determined to "civilize" the Indians and of army officers who hoped to curb the Indians' depredations. In 1867–68 the Peace Commission toured the West to meet with Indian leaders and negotiate treaties. A major goal of the Peace Commission was to confine the Indians to two large reservation areas—one to the north and one to the south of the route of the Union Pacific Railroad. In 1867 the commission signed treaties with the Southern Cheyenne and Arapaho, the Kiowa, the Comanche, and the Kiowa-Apache. These peoples agreed to relocate to two large reservations on lands recently taken from the Five Civilized Tribes in what is now western Oklahoma. In 1868 the government agreed to abandon its forts on the Bozeman Trail, and Red Cloud and other Sioux leaders agreed to remove to a huge reservation west of the Missouri River in Dakota Territory. Similar treaties were negotiated with the Northern Cheyenne and Arapaho in Wyoming Territory, with the Crow, Shoshone, and Bannock in Idaho Territory, and with the Ute in Colorado Territory. These treaties did not end the conflict in the West, however. The Indians often refused to stay on their reservations. But now the government could cite the treaties as grounds for using force to make them return.

(continued on page 65)

IMAGES OF CHANGE

For centuries, the Indians of the Great Plains have used paintings to celebrate the exploits of warriors. In prehistoric times, they painted such images with vegetable dyes on cave walls and on buffalo hides. In the 19th century, after non-Indian explorers introduced Plains Indians to pencils, pens, and watercolors, the artists began to employ these materials to create drawings and paintings on cloth and paper.

The subject of these Indians' art also changed with the coming of whites. Although illustrations of battles remained popular, most created by Indians after the mid-19th century depicted conflicts with U.S. soldiers rather than intertribal warfare. In the late 19th century, when the Plains wars ended, many Indian painters began to represent reservation life. The subject of their illustrations reflected the influence of non-Indians, but the form of the images did not. The simple linear figures they used were firmly a part of an artistic tradition established by Indian cave painters long ago.

Painting by Yellow Nose, 1880. The Cheyenne artist shows himself on horseback attacking an enemy.

*The retreat of U.S. Army captain Marcus Reno's
battalion during the 1876 Battle of Little Bighorn,
in which Sioux and Cheyenne forces defeated troops
led by General George Custer. This drawing was
made in the late 19th century by Sioux artist Amos
Bad Heart Buffalo, whose father fought in the
battle.*

*A painting on canvas by Kills Two, an Oglala
Sioux, depicting a conflict between General Custer and Sioux leader Crazy Horse.*

A drawing on paper of a Cheyenne tapping a U.S. soldier on the head with a lance. This feat—known as counting coup—was considered a greater act of bravery than killing an enemy.

This Teton Sioux calendar, or winter count, was painted on a 35-by-36-inch piece of muslin and records the period from 1798 to 1922. Every winter, a record keeper would add a new image to the cloth to represent the most significant event that had occurred during the previous year.

The winter count's image for 1866 depicts a U.S. Army soldier threatening Sioux leader Gall with a bayonet.

This detail shows Sitting Bull shaking hands with a soldier in 1876, the year of the Battle of Little Bighorn.

The event representing 1898 is the hanging death of three Sioux convicted of murdering whites.

Between 1875 and 1878, the government imprisoned at Fort Marion in St. Augustine, Florida, 72 Indian men whom it considered the instigators of recent conflicts on the Plains. The soldiers at the fort gave the Indians pencils and paper, with which they created hundreds of drawings that were then sold to tourists.

Bear Heart, the most prolific artist among the Fort Marion inmates, drew from memory this 1876 illustration of an agent distributing goods on the Cheyenne reservation.

On the parapet of St Marion next day after arrival

An 1876 drawing by an artist named Zotom of the prisoners looking out at the Atlantic Ocean. These Plains Indians had probably never seen the ocean before they arrived in Florida.

A classroom at a school for the Fort Marion inmates, drawn by Zotom in 1876. The volunteer teacher, Laura Gibbs, taught the prisoners to read, write, and speak English.

(continued from page 56)

Another issue that arose during this time involved the BIA. In 1848, when the Mexican War ended, Congress created the Department of the Interior to supervise the vast territory that Mexico ceded to the United States. The department was also placed in charge of the Indians in this area. As a result, the BIA, which had been a branch of the War Department since its inception in 1824, was transferred to the Department of the Interior. But conflicts between Indians and settlers caused Congress to rethink the arrangement, especially after the Civil War, which left a surplus of army officers. These men could be placed in charge of the Indian reservations if the BIA was returned to the War Department. The change never came about, but Congress debated the issue strenuously until the 1880s. By this time most Indians were confined to reservations, which made it unlikely that any more major Indian uprisings would occur.

Among those most opposed to military rule of the Indians were humanitarians, church leaders, and philanthropists who believed the key to pacifying the Indians lay in education, missionary work, and honest dealing by civilian agents. These reformers managed to win the support of President Ulysses S. Grant, and in 1869 he inaugurated the Peace Policy. It consisted of two interrelated reforms. One was the establishment of the Board of Indian Commissioners. The other was the decision to staff Indian agencies with persons nominated by the major churches. Both these moves were intended to root out corruption in the BIA, chiefly among agents who mishandled funds and supplies, and to provide more enlightened leadership at the agency level.

The Board of Indian Commissioners comprised a group of wealthy philanthropists and businessmen appointed by the president. Candidates were suggested by various Protestant denominations, and the first board consisted of 10 members, including Henry S. Lane, former Indiana governor and U.S. senator; William E. Dodge, a New Yorker with interests in mining and railroads; and John V. Farwell, a Chicago merchant. The group received instructions from Ely S. Parker, Grant's commissioner of Indian affairs. He urged them to visit as many Indian sites as possible and to compile a list of suggestions for improving their conditions.

The board's primary responsibility was to assure that Indians received the goods promised them by their treaties with the U.S. government. Soon, however, the board accepted a greater challenge and suggested changes that would overhaul federal Indian policy. One recommendation, referred to as the "distribution of land in severalty," called for an end to the traditional Indian system of communal landholding. It proposed instead that Indians should be given individual plots of land on their reservation. The board also called for legal recognition of Indians as the government's wards, that is, as people the government was responsible for

An 1890 cartoon satirizing the widespread corruption of Indian agents. The agent pictured holds bags of annuity money but has given the Indian only a small package marked "starvation rations."

protecting. The board urged the government to educate Indians, "civilize" them (which meant, among other things, converting them to Christianity), and guide them toward economic well-being—all for the purpose of making the Indians prosperous citizens of the United States.

These ideals motivated a change in the way agents were selected. The Grant administration began what was known as the "Quaker policy," so named because it had first been discussed at a conference of Quakers in 1868. This policy called for Indian agents to demonstrate high character and strict morality. It went into effect in 1869, when the board determined that a number of churches should be asked to submit names of suitable people for jobs as agents. By 1872, 100 different agencies were staffed by church officials, predominantly Methodists, Quakers, Presbyterians, Episcopalians, and Catholics, although Baptists, Dutch Reformed, Congregationalists, and Unitarians were also represented.

For all the idealism and good intentions of Grant's policy, it failed to achieve its goal of transforming the Indians into "civilized" farmers. There were several reasons for this failure. For one, the churches could not recruit enough men to accept posts on reservations. For another, screening the applicants who did apply was an uncertain business. As before, corrupt agents slipped through the cracks. Those who did prove to be men of "high Christian character," as the recruiters had hoped, often possessed more religious zeal than practical skills. In addition, squabbles between various denominations for control of certain agencies led to disagreements. By 1882, no churches remained in the program.

Another long-standing federal Indian policy came to an end in the late 19th century. In 1871, Congress decreed that it would no longer negotiate treaties with Indian groups. The Indians had become so weak that many politicians saw no need for making arrangements with them as if they were foreign powers. Also, the House of Representatives, which appropriated all annuities, had grown resentful of being excluded from the actual negotiations, a responsibility that the U.S. Constitution placed firmly in the hands of the president and the Senate. Treaties gave way to "agreements," which both the Senate and the House could negotiate.

This development raised a new question. How was the federal government to deal with the many Indian groups that had never signed treaties and thus had never been guaranteed ownership of certain lands and protection of certain rights? Congress upheld the land claims made by many of these Indians. But in some cases Congress refused to act, and presidents began a new practice. They "withdrew" lands from the public domain—that is, made

Crow Dog, who the territorial court of Dakota sentenced to death for the murder of Chief Spotted Tail. He was freed when the Supreme Court ruled in 1883 that the lower court had no jurisdiction over crimes committed by one Indian against another.

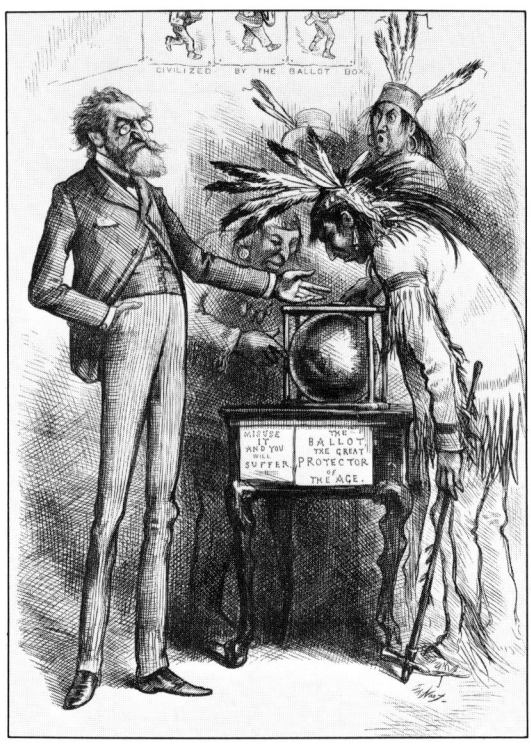

This political cartoon from the 1880s urged Secretary of the Interior Carl Schurz to give Indians the right to vote as "the cheapest and quickest way of civilizing them."

them off limits to whites—and turned them over to Indians whose land claims were not already recognized either by treaty or by congressional agreement. The legal validity of these "executive order reservations" was widely questioned in the late 19th and early 20th centuries, and today the question of Indian jurisdiction is being tested in the courts.

In the 1880s, federal power over reservation Indians grew sharply after a pair of decisions by the Supreme Court.

The first was in the case of *Ex parte Crow Dog* (*ex parte*, a Latin term meaning "from one side only," refers to a case in which only one side argues). Crow Dog was a Brule Sioux convicted of murdering another Indian, Chief Spotted Tail, and sentenced to death by the territorial court of Dakota. Crow Dog appealed the sentence, and on December 17, 1883, the high court ruled that Congress had established no jurisdiction over crimes committed by one Indian against another. Crow Dog was freed.

There was widespread outrage among legal and government authorities, and in 1885, Congress passed the Major Crimes Act. It gave federal courts jurisdiction over cases of murder, manslaughter, rape, assault with intent to kill, arson, burglary, and larceny, when these crimes were perpetrated by one Indian against another. For the first time in history, the United States asserted its authority over what had previously been considered the internal affairs of Indians on their own lands. Congress's authority was upheld by the Supreme Court in 1886 in *United States v. Kagama*. This decision held that Indians were members of "not a State or nation" but of "local dependent communities." It allowed for unlimited federal interference in Indian affairs.

In 1884 the courts delivered yet another surprise. It was an outgrowth of the Fourteenth Amendment to the Constitution, which guaranteed the rights of citizenship to newly freed slaves. The amendment had previously been ruled inapplicable to Indians, although many reformers assumed that if "civilized" Indians left their reservation they would be considered citizens and afforded the right to vote. This turned out not to be the case, however, for John Elk, an Indian who had abandoned his tribe to settle in Omaha, Nebraska. He tried to register, and later to vote, but was turned away from the polling station on the grounds that as an Indian, he was not a citizen of the United States. Elk's case was immediately taken up by several Indian defense groups and eventually came before the Supreme Court. It ruled in *Elk v. Wilkins* that Elk's separation from his tribe and residence among whites did not, in and of itself, make him a citizen. The court held that Indians could qualify for citizenship only if Congress passed an act specifically providing for their naturalization.

These court cases and the fate of Indians on the reservations led reformers to push for allotment of tribal lands, the notion originally embraced by the Board of Indian Commissioners. In the 1880s the policy of allotment gathered momentum. Its proponents argued that as the population of the United States continued to grow, whites would resent the few Indians who owned huge quantities of land and, by and large, made no effort to develop them. In time, the white population would wrest the land away. The only way to protect the Indians was to give the head of each family a fixed amount of land equal to what most whites had. If any land was left over after every Indian on a reservation had been given an allotment, the surplus could then be sold to land-hungry whites. This would satisfy them and create revenue that could be used to "civilize" the Indians, who would then become citizens and able to protect themselves with the vote.

Unfortunately, the reformers' faith in the power of private ownership of property, agriculture, and citizenship blinded them to the consequences of their flawed vision, as the next phase of Indian history would show. ▲

Indians applying for inclusion on a tribal roll in Muskogee, Indian Territory, circa 1890.

THE DAWES ACT
AND ITS FAILURE
1887 TO 1934

In 1887, Congress passed the General Allotment Act, also known as the Dawes Severalty Act, or Dawes Act, after its sponsor, Massachusetts senator Henry L. Dawes. Its purpose was to open the way for Indians to enter mainstream American society, and its premise was that they could do this more easily if they became independent landholders.

The Dawes Act covered two main issues. One was land. The act authorized the president to break up a reservation held in common by the members of a tribe into small allotments that would then be parceled out to individual Indians. Originally, allotments were to be distributed only to men, but in 1890 the act was amended to award them to women as well. Thereafter, each head of a family would be entitled to a minimum of 160 acres; unmarried persons over 18 and orphans under 18 would receive 80 acres; and children living with their parents would be given 40 acres. The allotments could be doubled in size in areas where the reservation land was suitable only for grazing rather than for farming.

The other major issue addressed by the Dawes Act was Indian citizenship. The act decreed that all Indians who received an allotment or left their tribal residence in order to live among non-Indians automatically became U.S. citizens, subject to the laws of the state or territory in which they resided. This raised a problem: taxes. As citizens, Indians would have to pay taxes on their land, which could bankrupt them if they were not able to make the land profitable. For this reason, the Dawes Act provided that the allotments would be held in trust by the federal govern-

Massachusetts senator Henry L. Dawes, the leading proponent of the allotment policy.

ment for 25 years. During this period the Indians could not sell the land and it could not be taxed. By the end of this trust period, the government hoped allottees would have learned how to farm and how to protect themselves from whites eager to get their hands on the Indians' lands. The government would then issue the allottees formal deeds, and they would acquire the obligations and rights of other landholders.

When the Dawes Act went into effect, reformers praised it lavishly. They and the government envisioned its passage as the beginning of the end of the "Indian problem" that had faced the nation since its inception. With the settlement of the West and the destruction of the game upon which many tribes depended, they believed the time had come for the Indians to settle down on farms and live like other Americans. Twenty-five years, or about one generation, was considered enough time to bring Indians into the American mainstream if the government provided education and instruction in farming. Sometime in the early 20th century, the reformers confidently predicted, the federal government would at last be out of the "Indian business."

In truth, the Dawes Act marked the end of Indian independence. One reason was that as individual Indians became citizens and landholders, their tribal governments lost legal control over both them and the former reservation land. Congress had already reduced tribal control in 1885 by passing the Major Crimes Act, which stated that certain crimes committed by one Indian against another came under the jurisdiction of the U.S. government. But after a reservation was parceled out as allotments, the new owners were subject to territorial and state laws as well.

Another problem with allotment was that it resulted in Indians losing much of their land. The Dawes Act provided that if there was land left over after all the Indians on a reservation had received an allotment, the government could sell the surplus to settlers. Knowing this, non-Indian homesteaders began to clamor for the government to break up reservations as quickly as possible. Some settlers simply violated the law and seized Indian lands outright, sometimes committing murder to gain it. Between 1887 and 1934, when the allotment policy was suspended, the amount of land owned by Indians fell from 138 million to 48 million acres. Most of the property that Indians retained was reservation holdings that were never allotted, and about half of this was desert or near-desert land unsuitable for farming.

A third problem with allotment was its failure to transform Indians into "civilized" farmers. Most Indians did not want to take up agriculture. The minority who did want to farm could seldom afford to buy plows, draft animals, or seed, or to drill water wells. Moreover, many allotted lands were located in areas not suitable for farming, as whites who purchased the surplus lands soon learned. Other areas required irrigation, an expensive investment that the government shied from making.

The difficulties did not end there. Many allotments fell to Indians who were too old, too young, or too feeble to farm. This was the case for the Winnebago Indians, who lived in Nebraska. In 1890 their agent reported that 60 percent of their land belonged to persons incapable of farming it. Additional acres went to waste because they were owned by children who were sent to Indian boarding schools far away from their homes. Some of this unused land was farmed illegally by whites.

In 1891 the Dawes Act was amended to allow allottees to lease their land to non-Indians for 3 years for farming and grazing and 10 years for mining if the secretary of the interior approved the arrangement. At first, tight restrictions limited this option to Indians who could not farm their allotments "by reason of age or other disability." But as whites hungered for land, the restrictions loosened. In 1894, "inability" to farm was added to "age" and "other disability"; the 3-year farming or grazing lease was upped to 5 years, and 10-year leases could be issued not only for mining but also for "business purposes," meaning just about anything.

The inheritance of allotments created still another problem. Some Indians died before the trust period on their land had ended. Many left no wills, and their property was divided among their heirs. The more heirs a deceased allottee had, the smaller the plot inherited by each. Eventually, allotments were divided and subdivided so frequently that few Indians owned enough land to make it productive. To solve this problem, Congress again amended the Dawes Act. Now when an Indian landowner died, his or her land could be sold to whites, and the proceeds of the sale could be divided among the heirs. The result was a familiar one. Indian lands were placed into white hands—for good.

Most of the reservations that were allotted were in Washington, Idaho, Montana, and North and South Dakota, states admitted to the Union in 1889 and 1890. Elsewhere, some Indians were spared the effects of the Dawes Act. For instance, the Five Civilized Tribes and certain smaller groups

(continued on page 76)

ALLOTMENT AND THE COMANCHE INDIANS

In 1887, under pressure from land-hungry white constituents, the U.S. Congress passed the General Allotment Act, also known as the Dawes Severalty Act, or Dawes Act. Under the terms of this law, communally owned Indian reservations could be divided into small parcels, or allotments, one of which would be given to each tribe member. The act also stated that if any land were left over after all Indians had received their allotments, the "surplus" land could then be sold to whites. The congressmen believed that if Indians became landowners, all differences between whites and Indians would be resolved because Indians would gradually become part of mainstream society. Many tribes, however, had no such desire and made great efforts to block the allotment of their lands.

One of the tribes that fought hardest to escape allotment was the Comanche Indians of Oklahoma. The Comanche, who had fought intruders on their land for centuries, had been among the very last of the Plains tribes to surrender to the U. S. government's demand that they be confined to a reservation. Indeed, the final surrender by Comanche leader Quanah Parker did not occur until 1875, less than 15 years before allotment was implemented on their reservation.

The Comanche had several factors in their favor in their fight against allotment. Quanah Parker had many friends in Washington because he had earlier cooperated with U.S. officials by convincing tribe members to attend Christian churches and send their children to mission schools. For this reason, he was able to make demands on the allotment officials and thus gave the Comanche time to plan a strategy. The Indians were also aided by ranchers who leased at extremely low rates reservation lands on which to graze their cattle. The ranchers did not want to lose that bargain and so they also voiced their opposition to the allotment of the Comanche reservation.

After a delay of several years, in 1892 the U.S. government finally sent a commission, headed by David H. Jerome, to the tribe's reservation to compel the Comanche to agree to allotment. The Jerome Commission had to get approval from three-fourths of the men in the tribe in order to implement allotment, but the majority of them wanted no part of it. The commission therefore resorted to threats and dishonest acts in order to pressure enough Comanche to sign the allotment agreement it had drafted. Most of the Indians who signed it could not speak English and probably had no concept of private landownership, so it is unlikely that they understood the implications of their action.

By the end of 1892, the Jerome Commission had finally collected enough signatures to allot the Comanche reservation. However, the agreement was not ratified by Congress until 1900. In the intervening eight years, thousands of whites illegally took possession of reservation land. During this period, Quanah Parker led three delegations to Washington in an effort to persuade officials there to delay allotment even longer. The Comanche leaders succeeded in putting off its implementation until 1901 and gained a promise from the government that they could retain 480,000 acres of tribal property.

After the Comanche had received their allotments, a lottery was held in July 1901 to allocate the "surplus" reservation land. The government had divided it into 13,000 farms, for which 165,000 whites had applied. The applicants who did not receive farms continued to demand land, resulting in another lottery in 1906, during which the Comanche's 480,000 communally owned acres were sold illegally. In only two centuries, Comanche territory had been reduced from a vast domain that had provided the tribe with abundant resources to just a few individually owned Indian farmsteads.

The 1897 Indian delegation to Washington, D.C., led by Comanche chief Quanah Parker (far left). The group sought to overturn the allotment plan outlined in the 1892 Jerome Agreement.

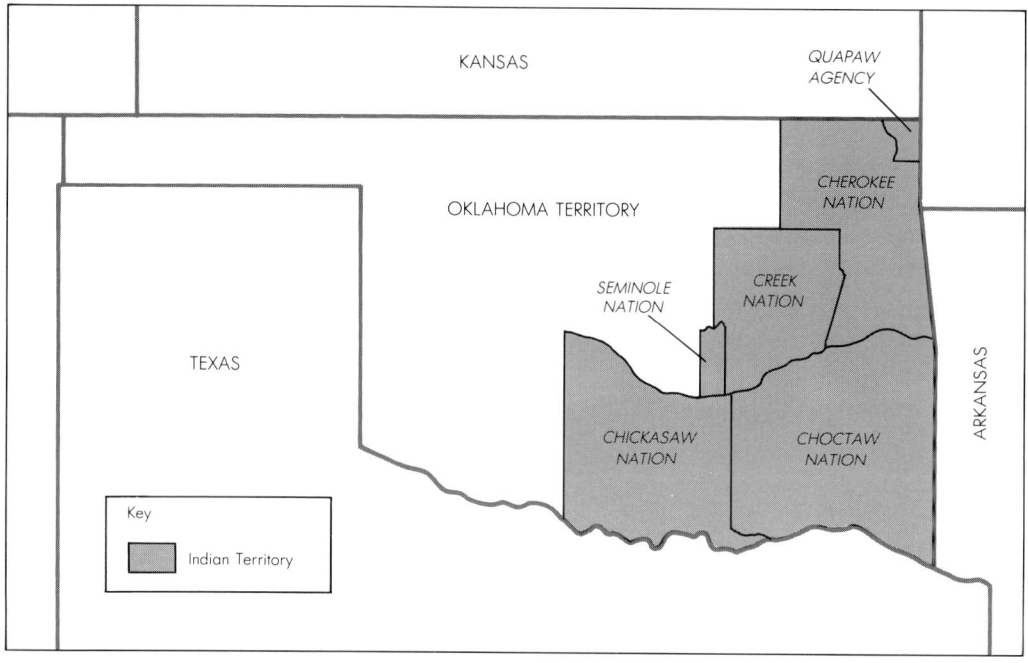

KANSAS

QUAPAW
AGENCY

CHEROKEE
NATION

OKLAHOMA TERRITORY

SEMINOLE
NATION

CREEK
NATION

TEXAS

ARKANSAS

CHICKASAW
NATION

CHOCTAW
NATION

Key

Indian Territory

(continued from page 73)

in Indian Territory, including the Osage and the Miami, were specifically exempted from the act because of provisions made in earlier treaties. Many Indians in New Mexico and Arizona were also spared, largely because those territories did not become states until the early 20th century. There was less pressure to allot reservations in territories than in states: Territories had no local governments that their white inhabitants could badger to open Indian land for non-Indian settlement.

In the late 1890s, as Oklahoma prepared for statehood, new legislation imposed allotment upon those tribes that had been exempted from the Dawes Act. In 1901 the members of the Five Civilized Tribes were granted citizenship. Whites in Oklahoma, which joined the Union in 1907, pressured Congress a year later to lift all restrictions on the sale of lands belonging to these tribes, precipitating a frenzy of selling.

The Dawes Act brought another old issue to light. In 1802, Congress had authorized Thomas Jefferson and all subsequent presidents to limit the sale of alcoholic beverages to Indians—in order to protect them. But once Indians were given allotments, this presidential power came under attack. Allotted Indians were now landholding citizens, and therefore, it was argued, they were entitled to whiskey if they wanted it. In 1905 the Supreme Court agreed. It declared that allotted Indians, as citizens, could no longer be considered wards of the government. Consequently, they could not be denied the right to purchase liquor.

The decision alarmed Congress, which in 1906 enacted the Burke Act (named for Congressman Charles H. Burke), another amendment to the Dawes Act. It provided that allotted Indians would not become citizens until the end of the trust period on their land. Before then they were subject exclusively to federal, rather than state, authority. In consequence, Indians, whether they had allotments or still resided on tribally owned reservations, would continue to be under the jurisdiction of the BIA. This was contrary to the expectations of reformers, who be-

lieved the Dawes Act would eventually render the bureau powerless.

The framers of the Burke Act also recognized that some Indians would be ready to manage their affairs sooner than others. For this reason the act empowered the secretary of the interior to issue land titles to individual Indians he deemed "competent" to handle their own affairs before the 25-year trust period had ended.

The low point for the Indians in the drive to force allotment on them came in the early 20th century, when the Kiowa and Comanche Indian reservation in Oklahoma was allotted and the government prepared to sell the surplus lands. The treaty that created the Kiowa and Comanche reservation con-

The members of the Dawes Commission, which negotiated allotment treaties with the Five Civilized Tribes. The commission is shown at the signing of a treaty with the Cherokee.

tained a clause stating that no part of the land could be sold unless three-fourths of the adult males of the tribes agreed. Federal agents negotiated an agreement that was approved by only a few Kiowa and Comanche leaders. Nonetheless, Congress accepted the agreement and opened the reservation to whites.

Lone Wolf, a Kiowa, challenged this action by bringing suit against the government. In 1903, *Lone Wolf v. Hitchcock* reached the Supreme Court. The Court ruled that Congress had virtually unlimited authority over Indian relations and also could void or break treaties without Indian consent if it deemed it

"in the interest of the country and the Indians themselves, that it should do so." Thereafter, Indians had no legal means of preventing Congress from ordering the breakup of reservations.

Beginning in 1915, the BIA dismantled a key provision of the Dawes Act by ordering that the 25-year trust period could be shortened in the case of Indians who were judged competent to handle their own affairs. Competent Indians, according to the BIA, included all those 21 or older who had graduated from the sixth grade and all those whose ancestry was less than one-half Indian. This decision forced thousands of Indians to accept full ownership of

Navajo Indian Tom Toslino when he arrived at the Carlisle Indian Industrial School (left) and after he had attended the institution for three years. Before-and-after photographs such as these were used by officials at Carlisle as evidence of their success in "civilizing" their Indian students.

Indian students in a classroom in Genoa, Nebraska, in the late 19th century.

their allotment. Many soon lost them to white buyers or tax collectors.

Aside from land allotment, education was the most important feature of federal policy in the late 19th and early 20th centuries. Reformers long held that Indians should be sent to English-language schools, where they would be taught as non-Indian Americans were. This seemed even more crucial after allotment, because Indians would have to be able to speak, read, and write English and perform basic mathematical tasks in order to manage their own affairs and deal successfully with whites. In 1887, when Congress passed the Dawes Act, only 10,000 out of 350,000 school-age Indian children attended

schools of any kind. By 1900 the number of students had climbed to 26,000, but most were enrolled in Indian boarding schools where they spent only half the day in class; the rest of the time they worked as janitors, launderers, or other maintenance workers at their schools.

In the early 1900s, the government decided that Indian students should be enrolled in local public schools. It hoped this alternative would cost less than sending them away to boarding school and might also prove more effective in detaching Indian students from their traditional ways and culture. White adults, however, often objected to Indian children sitting beside their own in the classroom. Even when

A group of Seminole Indians in Miami, Florida, voting for the first time, 1921.

whites relented, Indian children often suffered at school. They were ridiculed by classmates and teachers alike because they were poor, knew little English, and were often older than other children at the same grade level. Many Indian students consequently attended school infrequently or refused to go to school altogether.

In 1920 the federal government adopted a policy of compulsory education. It gave Indian agents license to act as truant officers and force children to attend school, often in boarding schools far from their home. This method was harsh but, to some extent, successful. By 1928 approximately 66,000 Indian children were enrolled in school, more than half in public schools. Few Indians received any schooling beyond the grade-school level, but this was not unusual for non-Indian students in rural America at the time. In 1928 only six Indian high schools established by the government provided high school courses.

The move to educate Indians led to an important—and alarming—discovery. School authorities soon found that poor health conditions existed in many Indian communities. The government responded in 1903 by ordering the first comprehensive survey of health conditions among Indians.

The report revealed that the Indian population were victim of malnutrition, unsanitary living conditions, and two diseases, tuberculosis and trachoma (an eye disease that leads to blindness). Congress allocated more funds to the reservations but not nearly enough. During World War I (1914–18), when many doctors and nurses left the reservations for better jobs elsewhere, the health-care system on the reservations collapsed.

In 1924 all Indians were awarded U.S. citizenship, partly in response to the contribution of Indian men who had distinguished themselves as soldiers in World War I. But the Citizenship Act was a formality that did little to improve the well-being of Indians.

Another development made a much bigger difference. In 1926 the Department of the Interior enlisted a private organization, the Institute for Government Research, to investigate the BIA. Two years later, the institute released a report, *Problems of Indian Administration*, commonly known as the Meriam Report, after its editor, Lewis Meriam.

The report made several recommendations. The agency should hire more Indian staff, pay its employees better, increase funding for health and education, and phase out boarding schools. The report also called for a Division of Planning that would "hasten agricultural advances, vocational guidance, job placement, and other aspects of economic development." The report faulted allotment and urged that the misguided policy be ended. The Meriam Report caused a stir in the federal government, and many of its recommendations went into effect in the next decade, when a crisis in the American economy led to drastic reforms in Indian policy. ▲

Secretary of the Interior Harold Ickes (seated), in 1935, signing the constitution of the Flathead Indians, the first tribe to establish a government according to the provisions of the Indian Reorganization Act. Behind him are six Flathead leaders and Commissioner of Indian Affairs John Collier.

THE
INDIAN NEW DEAL
1933 TO 1967

When the Wall Street stock market crashed in 1929, the entire United States was plunged into economic hardship, and those who were already poor, including Indians, got poorer. In 1932 the nation elected a dynamic president, Franklin D. Roosevelt, who promised the American people a New Deal and appointed many innovators to posts in his administration. One of the ablest was Commissioner of Indian Affairs John Collier.

Collier was born in Atlanta, Georgia, in 1884. He studied literature at Columbia University in New York City, psychology at the College de France in Paris, and social work with a private teacher, Lucy Graham Crozier, who fired her pupil's enthusiasm for public service. In 1920 he visited the Taos Indian Pueblo in New Mexico's Rio Grande Valley. He was so impressed by

the community that he became a fervent admirer of Indian culture and a fierce advocate of Indian rights.

In 1923, Collier became a founding member of the American Indian Defense Association, a lobbying group based in Washington, D.C. As the group's executive secretary, Collier struggled for 10 years to improve the lot of Indians. In 1933, Roosevelt tapped Collier to head the BIA, and the new commissioner took office with a full agenda. Chief among his goals were ending the allotment of Indian land; the defense of Indians' religious freedom and civil liberties; the preservation and reinvigoration of tribal cultures and societies; the conservation and rehabilitation of Indian lands; federal loans for economic development of Indian reservations; the settlement of Indian claims against the federal government;

Commissioner John Collier, who initiated sweeping reforms in Indian policy during his tenure at the Bureau of Indian Affairs.

and the creation of special federal courts that would hear all cases involving Indian tribes. In short, Collier envisioned an end to the individualization of the American Indian and a return to tribalism.

Collier achieved many of his aims by making changes in the administration of the BIA. This meant, however, that subsequent commissioners could reverse his policies. To prevent that, Collier in 1934 approached Senator Burton K. Wheeler of Montana and Representative Edgar Howard of Nebraska with the draft of a bill that would make his policies permanent. Congress made a great number of changes in the draft and rejected outright some of Collier's

ideas, but finally passed the bill. This legislation—the Indian Reorganization Act of 1934 (also known as the Wheeler-Howard Act and as the Indian New Deal)—remains a milestone in federal Indian policy.

The Indian Reorganization Act, or IRA, contained three major provisions. First, it repealed the allotment provisions of the Dawes Act and pledged that the government would return to tribes all the lands that had once been within the boundaries of Indian reservations and had not yet been sold to whites. The act extended the trust period on allotments indefinitely, so that they could never be sold to whites. It also authorized a $2 million annual fund that would be used to buy up additional lands for Indian individuals and tribes, and established a program of Indian land rehabilitation and conservation.

Second, Collier's plan granted tribes the right to organize for the purposes of limited self-government and economic development. Tribes that took this initiative were guaranteed the power over their members that municipalities, or town governments, receive. The act also made limited funding available for the political organization of tribes and authorized tribes to incorporate and to manage their own property. The secretary of the interior had to approve all political and economic activities, a provision that extended the powers of that office.

Third, the act promised that qualified Indians would be given preference, without regard to civil service requirements, for positions in the BIA and that $250,000 would be appropriated annually for educational loans to Indian students.

Much to Collier's disappointment and chagrin, Congress refused to endorse provisions in his original draft of the bill that would have helped promote the preservation of Indian culture. Congress also eliminated his proposal for the establishment of special courts that would have observed Indian traditions and customs in decisions involving conflicts between the new self-governing Indian communities and state and local governments. Congress

rebuffed as well Collier's efforts to return allotted lands to tribal ownership and to extend tribal government to all Indian tribes.

Congress also inserted a stipulation in the IRA that called for the members of each tribe recognized by the government to decide by vote whether or not to accept the act's provisions. In addition, Congress excluded Indians living in Oklahoma and Alaska, on the grounds that they needed no protection. Finally, the legislators declined to create a forum to resolve all outstanding Indian claims against the government.

Collier accepted these setbacks and energetically set out to enforce the IRA.

(continued on page 88)

Navajo Indian John Benally teaching two women to read and write the Navajo language in 1940. Bilingual education for Indians was one of Collier's innovations.

TERMINATION AND THE MENOMINEE INDIANS

During the 1940s, several Republican members of the U.S. Congress devised a plan that would allow the federal government to end its financial relationship with American Indians. Under this plan, known as termination, federal officials could decide that a particular tribe was capable of handling its own business affairs; the government could then cease paying annuities or providing services, such as health care and education, that it had promised the group in treaties negotiated years earlier. The members of terminated tribes also would have to begin paying taxes on their land and income.

One of the first tribes the government deemed ready for termination was the Menominee of Wisconsin. In 1951, the federal government awarded the tribe $8,500,000 on the condition that it stop pursuing several lawsuits against the United States. The settlement seemed to ensure the economic well-being of the Menominee people. As a result, on June 19, 1953, a delegation of U.S. congressmen led by Senator Arthur V. Watkins of Utah arrived on the tribe's reservation to discuss the terms of their termination. To ensure the Indians' cooperation, Senator Watkins hinted that payment of the money the government owed them might be delayed indefinitely if the Menominee resisted termination.

Most of the 3,254 tribe members wanted to keep out of the termination process altogether. Indeed, some spoke no English at all and probably had little understanding of the implications of the plan. As a result, only a small group of 169 Indians, led by Menominee Tony Waupochick, approved the delegation's terms. Despite this minimal support, termination was set to go into effect on December 31, 1958.

The Menominee were given three years to prepare to take financial control over their tribal properties, which included a reservation and a lumber mill. The tribal government hurriedly formulated a plan to make the Menominee reservation into a county, which would place the tribal members, their businesses, and their properties under the jurisdiction of the state of Wisconsin.

The tribal government also created Menominee Enterprises, Incorporated (MEI) to oversee all reservation property and the mill. The corporation was supposed to be governed by the members of the tribe, all of whom had shares in it. But tribal control of the corporation was lessened greatly soon after termination.

In order to raise funds to pay state and federal taxes, MEI ordered all tribe members to purchase their homes from the company at a fixed rate. Because most tribe members had little money, they used their stock to pay

A Menominee couple, photographed in 1964, sit in their ramshackle two-room house. After the Menominee's tribal status was terminated, the once-prosperous Indians became poverty stricken.

for the land, thereby giving MEI total control over much of the Menominee's property. The corporation then sold a large portion of this property, including much of the tribe's traditional hunting and fishing territory, to non-Indians.

Termination proved disastrous to the Menominee in other ways as well. The unemployment rate in Menominee County became the highest of any in the state. The county's infant mortality rate also rose to three times that of the rest of Wisconsin. Before termination, the Menominee had used only $144,000 in federal funds; after termination, however, welfare services and poverty programs increased government costs to $2,357,000.

Termination, which the government had originally adopted to save federal money, had backfired completely. The experiences of the Menominee and other terminated tribes led the government to gradually abandon the policy in the 1970s. On April 23, 1975, less than 20 years after the termination of the Menominee, the government restored their official tribal status and returned their reservation to them.

(continued from page 85)

By the end of his tenure, in 1945, 92 tribes had adopted constitutions that defined their political powers and 71 had incorporated for economic purposes. Collier strove valiantly to preserve and enhance the remaining Indian landed estates and to encourage economic development on the reservations. Sometimes, especially in the Southwest, his measures bit into the incomes of Indians and aroused their ire. But Collier stayed firm.

He also won some late-round victories. Through Collier's efforts, Congress was persuaded in 1936 to pass the Oklahoma Indian Welfare Act, which extended some of the benefits of the IRA to the Indians of Oklahoma. Congress also approved the establishment of an Indian Arts and Crafts Board to help Indian artists sell their handicrafts. And Collier won support for a bill that enabled more Indian children to attend day schools near their homes or to en-

Pagago Indians registering for the draft in 1940 outside the San Xavier Mission in Tucson, Arizona.

Secretary of the Interior J. A. Krug, in 1950, signing a contract to allow the government to purchase 155,000 acres of land on the Fort Berthold Indian Reservation in North Dakota. The sale was made without the consent of the reservation's business council chairman, George Gillette, who weeps as he watches Krug.

roll in nearby public schools, some of which featured bilingual classes, another Collier innovation.

Funding for many of the IRA's programs ended when the United States entered World War II in December 1941. Other of Collier's plans were stalled when many Indian community leaders left their reservation to serve in the United States's armed forces. Ironically, Indian involvement in the war called into question the basic principles of the IRA. As Indian servicemen re-

turned home, many brought with them new ideas they had obtained through contact with non-Indian soldiers. Some decided to leave their reservations after having learned ways to earn a better living in non-Indian communities. Suddenly, Collier and the IRA came under attack for perpetuating the "un-American" idea that Indians were different from other citizens. Many of Collier's opponents in Congress used this argument in order to advocate slashing the BIA's budget. Amid a storm of pro-

An employee of the Public Health Service visiting an Indian mother and her child in 1965.

test, Collier resigned from his office in 1945.

Following Collier's resignation, some congressmen from the western states began to endorse a policy of "terminating," or separating, Indian tribes and reservations from federal responsibility. They took aim at several of Collier's programs. One was the Indian Claims Commission, a stepchild of the Indian New Deal, formed in 1946 to handle the backlog of Indian complaints against the federal government. Pro-

ponents of termination argued that the financial settlements resulting from these claims (they eventually totaled more than $800 million) gave the Indians a thick financial cushion and absolved the government from further responsibility. Congress next demanded that the government absolve itself from further economic or legal responsibility for Indian groups it deemed capable of taking care of themselves without federal aid. Subsequent legislation subjected Indians in several states—namely, California, Missouri, Nebraska, Oregon, and Wisconsin—to the criminal and civil jurisdiction of state courts. Finally, Congress urged that Indians be relocated from reservations to cities and towns. Many Indians volunteered to move, but most fled back to the reservation due to the pressures of discrimination and cultural isolation. Even so, the new policy began a large exodus that, as of the late 1980s, resulted in about half the Indian population living outside the boundaries of a reservation.

Luckily, termination did not halt the government's willingness to provide health and educational services to needy Indians. In 1946, shortly after Collier stepped down, the U.S. Public Health Service assumed responsibility for Indian health and education. Its funding has grown steadily.

In 1958 the Department of the Interior under President Dwight D. Eisenhower announced that no further action would be taken to terminate Indian tribes unless the Indians themselves requested it. Since then, federal policymakers have returned to the policies initiated by John Collier and have assisted Indian tribes in rebuilding their communities.

In the 1960s, two developments advanced the cause of Indians. Two presidents—John F. Kennedy and his successor, Lyndon B. Johnson—announced plans to end poverty in the United States. At the same time, the civil rights movement, which sought fair treatment for minority groups, came into its own. As a result, the federal government approved much larger sums than ever before for Indian reservations, especially in the areas of health, education, and welfare. It also funded new social programs. Some of these programs made loans available to individual Indians to start businesses or build homes. Funds also went to medical and educational facilities.

In those years, Indians gained access to new sources of financial assistance and became less reliant on the BIA. In the 1970s and 1980s, however, the depth of the Indians' dependence was painfully exposed. ▲

Indian activists occupying the island of Alcatraz, in San Francisco Bay, in November 1969.

CONTEMPORARY INDIAN POLICY
1968 TO THE PRESENT

Nineteen sixty-eight was a landmark year for American Indians. It was then that President Lyndon B. Johnson, in a message to Congress, ushered in the era of self-determination. The time had come, Johnson said, to "erase old attitudes of paternalism and [to] promote partnership and self-help." The goal of federal Indian policy must be "a standard of living for Indians equal to that of the country as a whole, freedom of choice—an opportunity to remain in their homeland, if they choose, without surrendering their dignity, and an opportunity to move to the towns and cities of America if they choose, equipped with skills to live in equality and dignity; full participation in the life of modern America, with . . . economic opportunity and social justice."

Johnson swiftly established the National Council on Indian Opportunity, an investigative committee chaired by Vice-president Hubert H. Humphrey and composed of federal officials and Indian leaders. Its purpose was to evaluate current programs and to develop strategies for including Indians in future policy-making. That same year, Congress passed the American Indian Civil Rights Act. It freed Indians from the legal jurisdiction of the states and returned control to the tribes, strengthened the existing system of reservation courts, and gave Indians more leeway than they had before in rejecting lawyers made available to them by the government for legal cases. This legislation was passed without the consent of the Indians, however, and some feared that as the civil rights of individual Indians grew the power of the tribes might shrink. But federal court decisions, such as *Santa Clara Pueblo v. Martinez* (1978), upheld the tribes' immunity against suits by individual Indians.

*Members of the American Indian Movement
(AIM) occupying a church during their
1973 takeover of the town of Wounded Knee
on the Pine Ridge Sioux Reservation in
South Dakota.*

The government's measures responded to the growing national awareness that Indians had been treated poorly and unfairly throughout the United States's history. Changes within the Indian community drove the point home. For instance, in Minneapolis, Minnesota, young urban Indians, many of whom had never lived on reservations, formed the American Indian Movement (AIM) in 1968. This militant group demanded that the government redress its past and present failures and called for a return to a treaty relationship between the tribes and the federal government.

In 1969, Indian activists, following the lead of the black civil rights movement, staged several protests. One of the most newsworthy occurred in October 1969, when Indians occupied Alcatraz Island, a former federal penitentiary located in San Francisco Bay, and called for the government to build an Indian cultural center there. The authorities resisted and the demonstration dragged on, weakened by dissension among the protestors and by waning public support. Some demonstrators held firm, however, for 19 months, until government officials removed them from the island.

Another protest occurred in 1972 when hundreds of Indians traveled to Washington, D.C., to participate in a protest march called the Trail of Broken Treaties—a name derived from the Trail of Tears. They met with Harrison Loesch, an assistant secretary of the interior under President Richard M. Nixon, but were not satisfied. They then boldly dramatized their grievances by seizing the BIA headquarters for seven days. They vandalized many offices and carried off or destroyed thousands of important documents.

Probably the most widely publicized Indian protest during this time was staged on February 27, 1973, by nearly 200 members of AIM. Led by Indian activist Russell Means, they converged on the town of Wounded Knee on the Pine Ridge Sioux Reservation in South Dakota, the site of an Indian massacre in 1890. There, on December 29, 1890, U.S. Army troops had slaughtered almost 200 Sioux men, women, and children. The point of the AIM protest was to voice complaints against tribal leaders who Means charged had been given excessive power by the provisions of the Indian Reorganization Act. Means and his followers held off the FBI and federal marshals for 71 days before backing down.

The federal government did not turn a deaf ear to these Indian protests. In fact, the late 1960s and early 1970s saw major reforms in federal policy. In 1969, Nixon appointed Louis Bruce,

who is of Sioux and Mohawk ancestry, to head the BIA. Bruce overhauled the agency by giving 14 of 20 top staff positions to Indians.

In May 1970, Bruce spelled out a new role for the BIA. Instead of managing Indians, it would now serve them. Tribes would have the option of taking over any or all BIA functions, with the full cooperation of the agency, and the agency would team up with Indian rights organizations to improve the lives of urban Indians.

Bruce's program was backed by President Nixon in a 1970 message to Congress. Nixon urged the lawmakers

President Richard M. Nixon, in 1970, signing a bill that gave the Taos Pueblo Indians title to more than 48,000 acres of land in New Mexico.

to renounce the policy of termination; return sacred lands in New Mexico that the government had taken from the Taos Indian Pueblo in 1906; empower tribes to administer federally funded programs on Indian reservations, including schools and medical facilities; authorize funding for enhanced legal assistance to tribes to prosecute their complaints against the federal government; elevate the office of commissioner of Indian affairs to the level of assistant secretary of the interior; and greatly increase funding for economic development and health programs on reservations.

In 1975 the Indian Self-Determination Act translated these concepts into law. During the 5 years after its passage, $200 million in federal appropriations were directly administered to tribes. In the same span, most of Nixon's proposals were written into the books. So was the Alaskan Native Claims Act, which settled Aleut, Eskimo, and Indian land claims in that area. Also at this time, the Menominee, who had been terminated in the 1950s, regained their official status as a tribe and their reservation in Wisconsin.

Hard times came in the 1980s. The election of President Ronald Reagan signaled a struggle for Indians as the conservative president slashed the budget for almost all the social programs that benefited them. The tribes retained their political control, but they had come to rely on federal economic assistance, which was diminished.

The 1980s saw few innovations in federal Indian policy. As Indian writer Vine Deloria observed in 1984, Congress seemed to have exhausted its interest in Indian matters and was content simply to fund existing programs. As in many other areas of controversy in modern American life, the federal courts became the battleground for conflicts between Indians and non-Indians.

Perhaps the most important courtroom victory for Indians dated back to the Trade and Intercourse Act of 1790, the first law to detail the federal government's responsibility for Indians. This law provided that no Indian lands could be taken from them except by a treaty with the United States. During the next 100 years it was commonly believed that this provision did not apply to the original 13 states; their existence, after all, predated not only this law but also the U.S. Constitution. Instead, lawmakers believed, the 1790 act applied only to the Indian country west of the original United States.

Another century passed before the issue was settled. In the 1970s, a case involving two Abenaki tribes, the Passamaquoddy and Penobscot of Maine, reached the Supreme Court. Its ruling invalidated several treaties signed by the tribes and the state of Maine because they violated the prohibitions of the Trade and Intercourse Act. In 1980, the state of Maine was ordered by Congress and the Supreme Court to pay the Indians $81.5 million in compensation

Norman Wilson, director of a federal program to improve Indian housing, surveying a home on the Rosebud Indian Reservation in South Dakota in 1971.

for the lands they had ceded. Soon Indians in Rhode Island, Massachusetts, and Connecticut filed similar suits. In Massachusetts the Indian claims were denied, but in Connecticut and Rhode Island, settlements were reached in which the Indians were granted land and damages.

The New England Indian cases paved the way for others involving Indian rights. In the Southwest, where water is scarce, Indians have won significant claims to water previously believed to belong to non-Indian users. Indians have since sued for water

claims in other desert states. In the Pacific Northwest, several Indian groups have secured the right to fish in areas outside reservation boundaries.

These gains have been balanced by setbacks, however. In the 1980s, courts have denied tribal claims to control non-Indians on Indian reservations, although tribes have retained the right to police their own members.

As the 21st century approaches, American Indians remain in an awkward predicament as the tenants of a land over which they were once sovereign. They remain, as well, at odds

(continued on page 103)

A NEW HOME FOR AMERICAN INDIAN HISTORY

When Europeans first arrived on North American soil in the 16th century, they came into contact with societies wholly new to them. These societies, the many Indian tribes of North America, and the objects the Indians made instantly became a focus of admiration, wonder, and scientific study—as they remain to this day. Unfortunately, the Indians and their possessions also inspired greed and cruelty.

During the past four centuries, Europeans, and later Americans, sought control over the land and resources of North America and in the process completely disrupted traditional Indian ways of life. Indeed, the traditions of some American Indian tribes have been lost forever. As a result, the only sources of information about how these peoples lived are the objects that they made for ceremonial and everyday use.

In the late 19th century, several American anthropologists convinced the U.S. government to fund a ground-breaking project. The researchers collected artifacts from the rapidly disappearing Indian societies of North America. Their work inspired many other scientists, businessmen, and adventurers to do the same. One of the foremost of these collectors was New York businessman George Gustav Heye. Heye began buying Indian artifacts in 1897, often purchasing every item he could from the villages he visited. One journalist quipped that "he hated to leave a single Indian with any clothes on."

In order to house his vast collections, Heye constructed the Museum of the American Indian/Heye Foundation in New York City in 1916. Although Heye viewed it more as a tax write-off than a research center, he did hire anthropological scholars to oversee the actual care of the collections. Heye was forced to sell a significant number of his artifacts following the stock market crash of 1929, but the museum still had the largest collection of objects from American Indian culture in the world.

Unfortunately, Heye did not exert the same energy in bringing Indian culture to the viewing public as he did in building his collection. His museum had exhibit space for less than five percent of its specimens. Since Heye's death, the museum's administrators have constantly tried to find a larger facility in which to display its unique collections. This was one of the main goals of anthropologist Roland Force, who was hired as the museum's director in 1977. Immediately after assuming this post, Force began petitioning the government of New York City for a new museum location. After many years of negotiations, he finally succeeded in gaining approval, on May 8, 1989, of a landmark plan—the Museum of the American Indian/Heye Foundation would become part of the Smithsonian Institution.

The agreement between the two institutions will eventually result in the establishment of the National Museum of the American Indian on the Mall in Washington, D.C., and in the installation of an exhibition center at the Old United States Custom House in New York City. A facility for conservation and storage of the collections will be constructed at the Smithsonian's Museum Support Center in Suitland, Maryland, outside Washington.

The decision to honor American Indians with a museum in the nation's capital heralds a new era of respect for and historical reconsideration of the Indian tribes of the United States. As Smithsonian Institution secretary Robert McC. Adams noted, "the prospect of creating a National Museum of the American Indian . . . is likely to alter beyond all expectation public understanding of American Indian people."

A late-19th-century Zuni earthenware water jar from Laguna, New Mexico—one of the more than 1 million objects in the collections of the Museum of the American Indian/Heye Foundation.

LOCATION OF FEDERAL AND STATE INDIAN RESERVATIONS TODAY

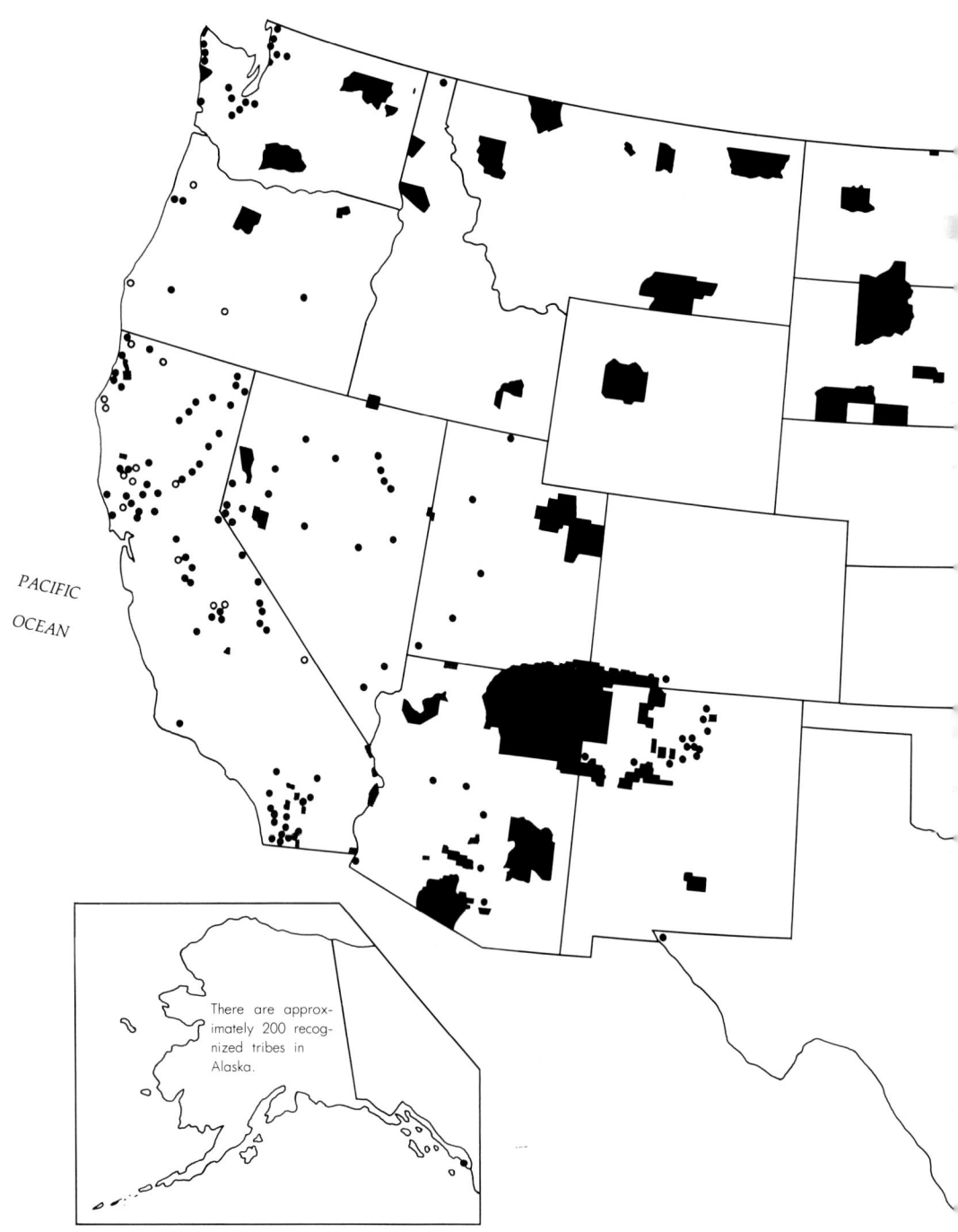

PACIFIC

OCEAN

There are approx-
imately 200 recog-
nized tribes in
Alaska.

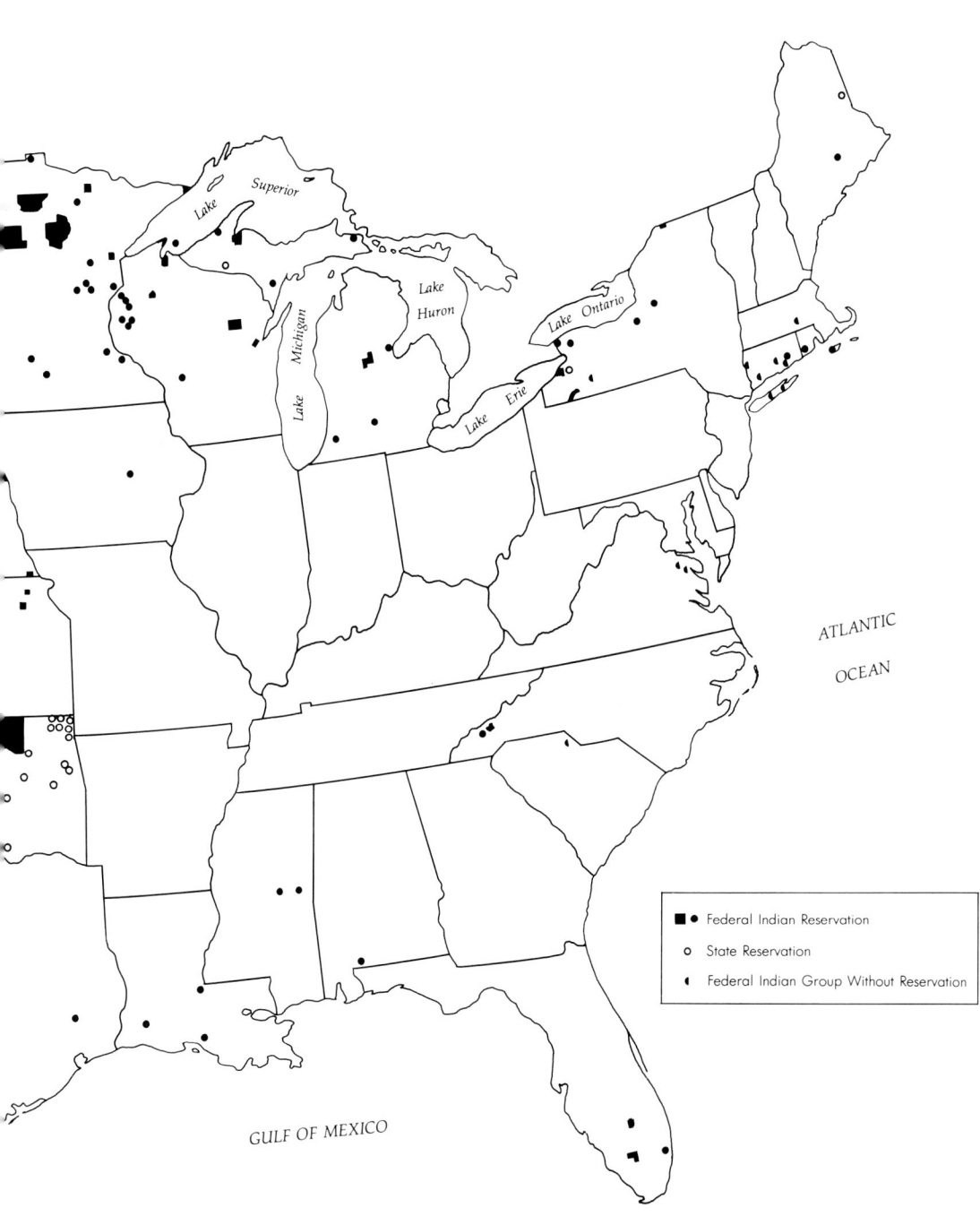

Lake Superior

Lake Huron

Lake Michigan

Lake Ontario

Lake Erie

ATLANTIC

OCEAN

■ ● Federal Indian Reservation

○ State Reservation

◀ Federal Indian Group Without Reservation

GULF OF MEXICO

A group of American Indian women demonstrating across the street from the United Nations during the "Long Walk for Survival" protest in 1980. The demonstrators called for the end of uranium mining on reservations.

(continued from page 97)

with many of their non-Indian neighbors. No less than the first European settlers, most modern Americans value property and uphold the virtue of their own culture. There is one difference, however, between past and present that gives solace to American Indians. Whites exhibit more tolerance than their ancestors of even half a century ago, and they seem less convinced that their way of life is the only way.

On more practical matters, Indians have weathered one crisis: There is no longer any danger that they will lose their reservation land. The trouble is that little of it can adequately support those who live on it. Thus, Indians continue to depend upon the federal government to supply them with crucial assistance. For now, there is little reason to think they will soon shed their dependence. The Indians' best hope is that the government will treat them generously, responsibly, and humanely—treat them far better, in other words, than it has so far. ▲

BIBLIOGRAPHY

Andrist, Ralph K. *The Long Death: The Last Days of the Plains Indians.* New York: Macmillan, 1964.

Deloria, Vine. *Custer Died for Your Sins: An Indian Manifesto.* Norman: University of Oklahoma Press, 1969.

Hagan, William T. *American Indians.* Chicago: University of Chicago Press, 1979.

Josephy, Alvin. *The Patriot Chiefs.* New York: Penguin, 1958.

Nash, Gary B. *Red, White, and Black: The People of Early America.* New Jersey: Prentice-Hall, 1974.

Nichols, Roger I. *The American Indian: Past and Present.* New York: Knopf, 1985.

Porter, Frank W., III. *The Bureau of Indian Affairs.* New York: Chelsea House, 1988.

Prucha, Francis Paul. *American Indian Policy in Crisis: Christian Reformers and the Indian, 1865–1900.* Norman: University of Oklahoma Press, 1976.

———. *American Indian Policy in the Formative Years: The Indian Trade and Intercourse Acts, 1790–1834.* Lincoln: University of Nebraska Press, 1970.

———. *The Great Father.* Lincoln: University of Nebraska Press, 1975.

Satz, Ronald N. *American Indian Policy in the Jacksonian Era.* Lincoln: University of Nebraska Press, 1975.

Spicer, Edward H. *A Short History of the Indians of the United States.* New York: Krieger, 1969.

Wilkinson, Charles F. *American Indians, Time, and the Law: Historical Rights at the Bar of the Supreme Court.* New Haven: Yale University Press, 1987.

GLOSSARY

agent A person appointed by the Bureau of Indian Affairs to supervise U.S. government programs on a reservation and/or in a specific region. After 1908 the title *superintendent* replaced *agent*. The British colonial government in the 1700s also referred to those who acted as liaisons with Indian groups as agents.

allotment U.S. policy applied nationwide in 1887 through the General Allotment Act (also known as the Dawes Severalty Act or the Dawes Act) aimed at breaking up tribally owned reservations by assigning individual farms and ranches to Indians. Allotment was intended as much to discourage traditional communal activities as to encourage private farming and the assimilation of Indians into mainstream American life.

American Indian Movement (AIM) A group formed in 1968 by urban Indian political activists in Minneapolis, Minnesota, whose goals were to gain fulfillment of U.S. treaty obligations to American Indians and to increase federal programs to support impoverished Indian families. AIM members staged a series of building takeovers, including one at Alcatraz prison, to focus media attention on the plight of American Indians.

annuity Compensation for land and/or resources based on terms of a treaty or other agreement between the United States and an individual tribe and consisting of goods, services, and cash given to the tribe every year for a specified period.

Bureau of Indian Affairs (BIA) A U.S. government agency now within the Department of the Interior. Originally intended to manage trade and other relations with Indians, the BIA now seeks to develop and implement programs that encourage Indians to manage their own affairs and to improve their educational opportunities and general social and economic well-being.

Carlisle Indian School A federally funded Indian boarding school in Pennsylvania that was in operation in the late 19th and early 20th centuries. Young Indians of many tribes who were sent there to assimilate into white culture.

cede To officially or formally surrender a possession. The treaties between the U.S. government and many Indian tribes often involved the cession of lands.

clan A multigenerational group having a shared identity, organization, and property based on belief in descent from a common ancestor. Be-cause clan members consider themselves closely related, marriage within most clans is strictly prohibited.

culture The learned behavior of humans; nonbiological, socially taught activities; the way of life of a group of people.

Department of the Interior U.S. government office created in 1849 to oversee the internal affairs of the United States, including government land sales, land-related legal disputes, and American Indian affairs.

Five Civilized Tribes A group of removed Southeastern Indian tribes, including the Creek, Choctaw, Chickasaw, Cherokee, and Seminole tribes, who shared adjacent reservations in Indian territory. The word *civilized* referred to the adoption by these tribes of many non-Indian customs.

French and Indian War A series of skirmishes fought between 1754 and 1763 in which England and France battled for control of land and resources in colonial North America. The French were aided in their fight with the British by the Algonquian-speaking Indian tribes of northeastern North America.

Great Plains A flat region in central North America between the western edge of the Great Lakes region and the Rocky Mountains. The Great Plains were covered by lush grasslands at the time of American settlement in the 19th century.

Indian Claims Commission (ICC) A U.S. government body created by an act of Congress in 1946 to hear and rule on claims brought by Indians against the United States. These claims stemmed from unfulfilled treaty terms, such as nonpayment for lands sold by the Indians.

Indian Reorganization Act (IRA) The 1934 federal law, sometimes known as the Wheeler-Howard Act, that ended the policy of allotting plots of land to individual Indians and encouraged the development of reservation communities. The act also provided for the creation of autonomous tribal governments.

Indian Territory An area in the south central United States to which the U.S. government resettled Indians from other regions, especially the eastern states. In 1907, the territory was incorporated into lands that became the state of Oklahoma.

Louisiana Purchase A vast tract of land purchased in 1803 by the United States from France during

Thomas Jefferson's presidency. Its boundaries were eventually defined as the Sabine, Red, and Arkansas rivers to the South, the contemporary Canadian border to the North, the Mississippi River to the east, and the Rocky Mountains to the west. Jefferson hoped to relocate Indians living east of the Mississippi River to this area in order to open their lands for settlement by non-Indians.

militia An army made up of citizens who are called into military service by a government.

mission A religious center founded by advocates of a particular denomination who are trying to convert nonbelievers to their faith.

Proclamation Line A boundary, defined by the British in the Proclamation of 1763 as the crest of the Appalachian Mountains, to the west of which non-Indian could settle until representatives of the British government had negotiated treaties with the Indian tribes occupying the region.

removal policy U.S. policy proposed by President Andrew Jackson and enacted by Congress as the Indian Removal Act of 1830. Removal policy called for the sale of all Indian land in the eastern and southern United States and the migration of Indians from these areas to territory west of the Mississippi River.

reservation, reserve A tract of land retained by Indians for their own occupation and use. *Reservation* is used to describe such lands in the United States; *reserve*, in Canada.

Sand Creek Massacre The Colorado territorial militia's slaughter of hundreds of Cheyenne and Arapaho Indians camped along Sand Creek in 1864 in what is now southeastern Colorado.

termination Federal policy to remove Indian tribes from government supervision and Indian lands from trust status, in effect from the late 1940s through the 1960s.

territory A defined region of the United States that is not, but may become a state. The government officials of a territory are appointed by the president, but territory residents elect their own legislature.

Trail of Tears The name given to the harsh journey taken by Cherokee Indians from their homeland in the southeastern United States to what is now Oklahoma in the 1830s.

treaty A contract negotiated between representatives of the U.S. government or another national government and one or more Indian tribes. Treaties dealt with the cessation of military action, the establishment of boundaries, terms of land sales, and related matters.

tribe A society consisting of several or many separate communities united by kinship, culture, and language, and other social institutions including clans, religious organizations, and warrior societies.

trust The economic relationship between the federal government and many Indians tribes, dating from the late 19th century. Government agents managed Indians' business dealings, including land transactions and rights to national resources, because the government considered Indians legally incompetent to manage their own affairs.

INDEX

Abenaki Indians, 19, 96
Adams, John, 38
Adams, John Quincy, 38
Agriculture, 20–21, 23, 33,
  41, 71–73, 81
Alabama, 34, 37, 40
Alaska, 85
Alaskan Native Land Claim
  Act, 96
Alcatraz Island, 94
Alcohol, 27, 38, 76–77
Aleuts, 96
Algonquin Indians, 19
Allotment, 46, 69, 71–73,
  76–77, 79, 81, 83–85;
  leasing of, 73; trust
  period on, 71–72, 77–78,
  84
Alphabet, Cherokee, 33
American colonies, 19–20,
  25; Indian policies of,
  20–21, 23, 25–26
American Indian Civil
  Rights Act, 93
American Indian Defense
  Association, 83
American Indian Movement
  (AIM), 94–95
Animals, 28, 73; buffalo, 13,
  18, 44, 51, 55; cattle, 18,
  49; horses, 18, 49
Annuities, 13, 46–47, 50, 67
Anthony, Scott J., 52
Apache Indians, 18, 47
Appalachian Mountains, 21,
  23, 25–27, 33
Arapaho Indians, 13, 47, 51,
  53, 56
Arizona, 18, 49, 76
Arkansas, 33, 41
Articles of Confederation,
  26, 29
Assimilation, 33, 41, 66–67,
  69, 71, 79
Atlantic Ocean, 21, 23
Atrocities, 49, 52–53, 94–95
Aztec Indians, 18

Bannock Indians, 56
Bilingualism, 89
Blackfoot Indians, 46–47
Black Kettle, 52

Blood Indians, 47
Bloodless Third, 52
Board of Indian
  Commissioners, 65, 69
Bosque Redondo, 49–50
Bozeman Trail, 56
Brant, Joseph, 26
Bruce, Louis, 95
Bureau of Indian Affairs
  (BIA), 13, 41, 45–46, 50,
  55, 65–67, 77–78, 81,
  83–85, 89, 91, 94–95;
  corruption in, 55, 65, 67
Burke Act, 77

Calhoun, John C., 41
California, 18, 44–45, 49, 91
California gold rush, 45
Canada, 18, 21, 23, 27,
  31–34
Carleton, James H., 49–50
Carolinas, 20, 23, 37
Carson, Kit, 49–50
Cayuga Indians, 26
Cheating, bribery, and
  intimidation, 13, 39
Cherokee Indians, 18, 25,
  32–33, 35, 37, 39–40,
  54–55
Cherokee Nation v. Georgia, 39
Cheyenne Indians, 13, 18,
  46–47, 51–52, 56
Chicago, Illinois, 34, 45
Chickasaw Indians, 32, 35,
  37, 39, 53–54
Chippewa Indians, 30
Chivington, John M., 51–53
Choctaw Indians, 32, 35, 37,
  39, 53–54
Christianity, 14, 29, 56,
  65–67
Church of Jesus Christ of
  Latter-day Saints. *See*
  Mormons
Citizenship, 38, 69, 71,
  76–77, 81
Citizenship Act, 81
Civil rights, 18, 83, 91,
  93–94; under
  Confederacy, 53
Civil War, 45, 47, 49, 53–55,
  65

Collège de France, 83
Collier, John, 83–85, 88–91
Colorado, 13, 51, 56
Colorado gold rush, 13, 47
Columbia University, 83
Comanche Indians, 46, 56,
  77–78
Confederation Congress,
  26–28
Connecticut, 20, 97
Connor, P. E., 52
Constitution, 29–30, 68, 96
Continental Congress, 25–26
Creek Indians, 32, 34–35,
  37, 39–40, 53–55
Crow Dog, 68
Crow Indians, 56
Crozier, Lucy Graham, 83
Cultural differences:
  between Indians and
  Europeans, 14–15, 29, 33;
  between tribes; 15, 18, 23

Dakota Territory, 56, 68
Dawes Act, 71–73, 76,
  78–79, 83
Deloria, Vine, 96
Denver, Colorado, 13, 52–53
Detroit, Michigan, 34
Dodge, William E., 65
Dog Soldiers, 51
Doolittle, James R., 55

Economic development, 81,
  83–84, 88
Education. *See* Schools
Eisenhower, Dwight D., 91
Elk, John, 69
Elk v. Wilkins, 69
England, 15, 18–21, 23,
  25–27, 31, 34, 41, 44
English language, 33, 79, 80
Eskimos, 96
Evans, John, 51–52
Everglades, 39
"Executive order
  reservations," 68
Ex parte Crow Dog, 68

Fallen Timbers, Battle of,
  31–32
Farming. *See* Agriculture

PICTURE CREDITS

AP/Wide World, pages 43, 82, 87, 92, 97; Cranbrook Institute of Science, pages 60, 61; Florida State Archives, page 40; The Thomas Gilcrease Institute of American History and Art, Tulsa, Oklahoma, pages 12, 15, 20, 36, 54; Illinois State Historical Library, page 35; Library of Congress, pages 27, 28, 31, 34, 38, 53, 56, 66, 68, 72; Museum of the American Indian/Heye Foundation, pages 19 (neg. #38321), 24 (neg. #39126), 30 (neg. #29699), 48 (neg. #31513), 67 (neg. #34816); Museum of New Mexico, pages 50, 51, 78; National Anthropological Archives, Smithsonian Institution, page 75 (neg. #44.453-a); National Archives, pages 55, 84; National Museum of Natural History, Smithsonian Institution, page 99 (neg. #86-3569); Nebraska State Historical Society, Solomon D. Butcher Collection, page 79; Newberry Library, Chicago, Illinois, cover, pages 56–59; Oklahoma Historical Society, page 79; Oklahoma Historical Society, Archives and Manuscript Division, page 43, 70; Photo Native American Painting Reference Library, Private Collection, pages 62–64; University of Kansas Libraries, Kansas Collection, page 47; University of Tulsa, McFarlin Library, Department of Special Collections, pages 46, 77 (Alice Robertson Collection); UPI/Bettman Newsphotos, pages 80, 85, 88, 89, 90, 94, 95, 102.

Maps (pages 2, 16, 17, 22, 32, 44, 76, 100, 101) by Gary Tong.

LAWRENCE C. KELLY is professor of American History at the University of North Texas, Denton, where he teaches 20th-century American history and federal Indian policy. He is the author of several books, including *The Navajo Indians and Federal Indian Policy* (1968), *Navajo Roundup: Kit Carson's Expedition Against the Navajo Indians* (1970), and *The Assault on Assimilation* (1983), and has written many articles dealing with American Indian history. His books have received awards from the American Association on State and Local History and the Texas Institute of Letters. He has received fellowships and research grants from the National Endowment for the Humanities, the Herbert Hoover and Harry S Truman Presidential Libraries, the National Science Foundation, and the School of American Research, as well as the American Philosophical Society, the Smithsonian Institution, and the Rockefeller Archives.

FRANK W. PORTER III, general editor of INDIANS OF NORTH AMERICA, is director of the Chelsea House Foundation for American Indian Studies. He holds a B.A., M.A., and Ph.D. from the University of Maryland. He has done extensive research concerning the Indians of Maryland and Delaware and is the author of numerous articles on their history, archaeology, geography, and ethnography. He was formerly director of the Maryland Commission on Indian Affairs and American Indian Research and Resource Institute, Gettysburg, Pennsylvania, and he has received grants from the Delaware Humanities Forum, the Maryland Committee for the Humanities, the Ford Foundation, and the National Endowment for the Humanities, among others. Dr. Porter is the author of *The Bureau of Indian Affairs* in the Chelsea House KNOW YOUR GOVERNMENT series.